HIV/AIDS DILEMMA!
CHRISTIAN RESPONSE TO HIV/AIDS

A TEACHING SERIES FOR THE CHURCH/ORGANIZATION

Dr. Sabelo Sam Gasela Mhlanga

WESTBOW
PRESS®
A DIVISION OF THOMAS NELSON
& ZONDERVAN

WestBow Press books may be ordered through booksellers or by contacting:

WestBow Press
A Division of Thomas Nelson & Zondervan
1663 Liberty Drive
Bloomington, IN 47403
www.westbowpress.com
844-714-3454

Scripture taken from the King James Version of the Bible.

Scripture taken from the New King James Version® Copyright © 1982 by Thomas Nelson. Used by permission. All rights reserved.

Scripture quotations taken from The Holy Bible, New International Version® NIV® Copyright © 1973 1978 1984 2011 by Biblica, Inc. TM. Used by permission. All rights reserved worldwide

ISBN: 978-1-6642-1819-2 (sc)
ISBN: 978-1-6642-1820-8 (e)

Print information available on the last page.

WestBow Press rev. date: 01/06/2021

CONTENTS

PREFACE

There is a God-honoring way to relate to God's image-bearers who have HIV/AIDS, and that way can be taught to Christians in the Church/Organizations. I would like to extend my profound gratitude to my supervisor, Dr. Danny Bowen, (A Medical Doctor), with his vast experience in Healthcare for more than forty-three years in the Medical Fraternity and as well as a great theologian, has brought his expertise, experience in this book. I pray that this book will benefit Christians, churches, and non-governmental organizations to respond to HIV/AIDS positive and other diseases battering humanity today in a God-honoring way.

My heart-felt thanks to my dear wife, Judith, and our children, Blessing, Shalom, Prosper, Emmanuel, and Joseph-Sam, Jr., my late father Joseph and late mother Josephine who gave me all their support spiritually, socially, and morally when they were still alive. Above all, I am thankful to God the Almighty, for giving me the strength and good health to serve Him and to write this book that will help thousands of people, churches, and organizations to respond to HIV/AIDS positive people. To God be the glory, honor, and praise from generations to generations and forever and ever.

— 1 —

INTRODUCTION

The dire situation faced by the people infected with HIV/AIDS and the way they are being treated in the societies requires a considered Christian response. The HIV/AIDS stigmatization has left HIV/AIDS victims hopeless and desperate about their condition and they yearn to be loved and treated with dignity and respect as they bear the image of God. Christians sometimes do not respond to HIV/AIDS victims with love. Those living with HIV/AIDS are confronted with isolation, stigmatization, and discrimination.

The situation is compounded by a tradition and culture with various myths related to HIV/AIDS that results in the exclusion of those infected with the disease. Yet, there is clear biblical teaching about how Christians should response to people who face all forms of suffering, such stigmatization, discrimination, and exclusion. There is a God-honoring way to relate to God's image-bearers who have HIV/AIDS in order for them to feel loved and cared for within the church and community. Therefore, it is imperative to design a teaching plan to change Christian attitudes and perceptions about the disease in order to change the societal response to HIV/AIDS positive people.

Although no specific texts in the Bible mention HIV/AIDS, an analysis of the texts in the context of leprosy highlight a similar stigma of HIV/AIDS that people face today. Robin Gill writes,

It is not possible to find, in the Bible, an exact parallel to stigmatization of those with HIV/AIDS: and yet within the biblical tradition, there are many examples that point to the way in which the stigmatized of the day were treated. We need to learn from the manner in which Jesus related to and responded to the stigmatized, for example, to the lepers, Samaritans, a menstruating woman, and those with physical and emotional disabilities.[1]

Jesus did not discriminate against anyone because of background, situation, condition or ethnicity. He met the needs of the people squarely as they needed him.

The church has been reluctant to respond in a compassionate way since HIV/AIDS was discovered in the mid-1980s. Avert Organization reports,

The first reported case of AIDS in Zimbabwe occurred in 1985. By the end of the 1980s, around 10% of the adult population was thought to be infected with HIV. This figure rose dramatically in the first half of the 1990s, peaking at 26.5% in 1997. However, since this point, the HIV prevalence is thought to have declined, making Zimbabwe one of the first African nations to witness such a trend. According to government figures, the adult prevalence was 23.7 percent in 2001, and fell to 14.3 percent in 2010.[2]

The stigmatization of people with HIV/AIDS was strongly felt in the churches and communities at its early discovery. It was regarded as the worst disease ever discovered. Christians justified themselves in

---

[1] Robin Gill, *Reflecting Theologically on AIDS: A Global Change* (London: SCM, 2007), 19.

[2] Avert.org, "HIV and AIDS in Zimbabwe," accessed June 3, 2015, www.avert.org/aids-zimbabwe.htm.

discriminating against HIV/AIDS victims. The church scorned the victims and believed it was God's punishment on immoral people. Some churches even excommunicated HIV/AIDS positive people from membership, claiming that they had brought shame and embarrassment to the church.

The disease created disparity in relationships in families, churches, and in communities. Some of the families quarantined and isolated HIV/AIDS victims to their own houses and fed them separately. The stigma of HIV/AIDS was similar to the stigma of lepers in Israel. Mary Ann Hoffman contends,

> HIV disease is not simply a physical entity. Rather, the impact of the disease is reflected in many other important ways, such as in emotional responses, copying strategies, self-image, and changes in life goals. However, the physical aspects of the disease often lead to the first awareness that something is amiss; then they become markers of the relentless progression of the disease.[3]

Although the response to HIV/AIDS positive people has changed over time, social discrimination still exists to this day.

A Christian response to HIV/AIDS is imperative and a teaching series for the churches, communities, and schools in the third world could help Christians respond to HIV/AIDS-positive people with compassion, championed by Christ. Brenda Almond is correct in her assessment that HIV/AIDS is more than a physical issue: "AIDS raises a number of ethical and social problems which must inevitably be confronted by the whole community, by people with AIDS and their relatives, and by those professionally involved."[4] Even though it is a physical, moral, social and emotional disease, there are God-honoring ways to relate to God's image-bearers who suffer from HIV/AIDS.

---

[3] Mary Ann Hoffman, *Counseling Clients with HIV Disease* (New York: Guilford, 1996), 7.

[4] Brenda Almond, *Aids: A Moral Issue* (New York: St. Martin's, 1990), 26.

A teaching series for the church is based on the Bible—the solid foundation for a biblical and theological Christian response to HIV/ AIDS. The understanding of being created in the image of God is fundamental to a Christian response to HIV/AIDS or any terminal disease patients. All humans are God-created beings. Being created in God's image, believers must uphold the dignity and respect of all human beings. At a minimum, a Christian response entails treating HIV/AIDS positive people with respect and dignity.

Exegesis of Respect Due Image-Bearers (Gen 1:26-28, KJV)

"And God said, let us make man in our image, after our likeness and let them have dominion over the fish of the sea" (Gen 1-26a, KJV). The deep understanding of man being created in the *image* of God and his *likeness* is important.

Being created in the image of God is a great honor to man because God applied himself to creation through man to bear his image. All human beings were created in the image of God; therefore, all due respect must be bestowed to image-bearers. Harmony and good relationship with God was broken because of sin through Adam and Eve, God's first image-bearers.

The Fall and the Consequences (Gen 3: 1-16, KJV)

The teaching plan begins with the fall in Genesis 3:1-16, KJV, in which there was a broken relationship between God and man. Man lost immortality through disobedience. In his providence, God's response to Adam and Eve's disobedience was remarkable. He clothed them in animal skins, which was an act of grace and a symbol of a future permanent solution for redemption. Fretheim gives an interesting analysis: "Even more, this God comes to the man and woman subsequent to their sin; God does not leave them or walk elsewhere. . . . God's response centers on their nakedness, not on their fear."[5] God has never left humanity alone, even though they sinned against him. He loved and cared for humanity, hence he responded to their needs.

The teaching plan examines the text and exegetes the implications and results of the fall. The significance of animal sacrifice before the permanent solution through Christ Jesus is also expounded. Before understanding redemption through Christ Jesus, one has to understand the fall that brought misery through disobedience to God's commands. Genesis 3:1-16, KJV, gives detailed information about the condition of man before the fall, the consequences of the fall, and God's plan for salvation. Developing a teaching series, with Genesis 3:1-16, KJV, as the backbone of the teaching series, enhances the understanding of the fall of man and the redemptive plan of God for humanity.

God's Redemption Plan for Humanity (John 3:16, KJV)

God did not leave man in his predicament of eternal death. In due time, he sent his only begotten Son, Jesus Christ, to redeem his own people. John 3:16, KJV, connects the fall of man to redemptive grace that came through Christ. Hebrews 10:4-7, NIV, says,

> It is impossible for the blood of bulls and goats to take away sins. Therefore, when Christ came into the world, he said: "Sacrifice and offering you did not desire, but a body you prepared for me; with burnt offerings and sin offerings you were not pleased." Then I said, "Here I am, it is written about me in the scroll I have come to do your will, my God."

God's redemptive plan for humanity is expounded in John 3:16,

---

[5] Terence E. Fretheim, *Genesis*, in. vol. 2 of *The New Interpreter's Bible Commentary in Twelve Volumes*, ed. L. Juliana Claassens and Bruce C. Birch (Nashville: Abingdon, 1994), 362.

NIV: "For God so loved the world, that he gave his only Son, that whoever believes in him should not perish but have eternal life."

His love is not confined to specific groups of people; instead, his love proceeds from the fact that he is the God of love (1 John 4:8, 16, NIV), Morris explains,

> The atonement proceeds from the loving heart of God. It is not something wrong from him. The Greek construction puts some emphasis on the actuality of the gift: it is not 'God loved enough to give,' but 'God loved so that he gave.' His love is not a vague, sentimental feeling, but a love that costs. . . . There are no Divine gifts apart from or outside the one-born Son.[6]

God showed his loved the world by sending his son into the world, but also gave him on the cross to be a ransom for many. First John 4:8, 16, NIV, is packed with all the attributes of God and the loving kindness he unleashes to all humanity who embrace his son for the forgiveness of their sins. The foundation for the love and care God has bestowed to all people who embrace Christ as their personal Lord and Savior. Consequently, Christ demonstrates his Father's love in his ministry on earth. An exegesis of John 3:16 NIV, reveals the depth and the essence of the sacrificial love. When Christ redeems his own people from their sins, he commissions them to spread the news to the whole world. The gospel has been handed over to the disciples of Christ to witness, teach, and preach to all people. In Matthew 28:18-20, NIV, Christ commands the disciples to carry out his mission to reach all peoples in the world.

---

[6] Leon Morris, *The Gospel according to John*, The New International Commentary of the New Testament, rev. ed. (Grand Rapids: William B Eerdmans, 1995), 203.

The Great Commission (Matt 28:18-20, KJV)

The Great Commission is God's call to Christians to respond with love and compassion to all the people to reach out to all the nations with the gospel. The text presents Christ's commission to all his disciples to go out and to make a difference in the world by making disciples of all nations, baptizing them in the name of the Father, and of the Son, and of the Holy Spirit, and teaching them to obey everything that he had commanded them. The passage connects Jesus Christ with his disciples after his death and resurrection, and he assures them that the two empires, heaven and earth, have been given to him by his Father: "All authority in heaven and on earth has been given to me" (Matt 28:18, NIV). He reestablished an intimate relationship with his disciples after they were scattered and living under fear after Christ's death; but the resurrection brought new hope. Now Jesus assured them that they should no longer be afraid because all authority in heaven and on earth was given to him. Donald Hagner concludes, "The passive verb assumes God as the acting subject: God has given Jesus this comprehensive sovereignty over the whole created order. Already in his ministry he had made statements about his authority."[7] It was the time to assure his disciples that he was alive. R. T. France writes,

> Jesus' declaration and commission which will conclude the gospel are introduced not by a simple 'Jesus said' but by a combination of three verbs: he "came to" them, "spoke to" them, and "said." This rather fulsome introductory clause not only emphasizes the climatic role of this speech but also responds to the disciples' hesitation: Jesus' "coming to" his frightened Disciples [is] an act of reassurance.[8]

---

[7] Donald A. Hagner, *Matthew 14-28*, Word Biblical Commentary, vol.33B (Dallas: Word, 1995), 886.

[8] R. T. France, *The Gospel of Matthew*, The New International Commentary on the New Testament (Grand Rapids: William B. Eerdmans, 2007), 1112.

The disciples needed that assurance and empowerment from the risen Christ. They would use the name of Jesus to preach, teach, witness, disciple, cast out demons, and stand against all the forces against God in the world.

The death and the resurrection of Jesus ushers a new paradigm of worldwide evangelism not limited to Israel. The direct commission is to all nations. Both the Jews and the Gentiles are included in the history of salvation. The Great Commission accomplishes four fundamental goals: (1) to baptize the new converts, (2) to make disciples of all nations, (3) to teach them to obey all the commands that he had commanded them, and (4) to give them assurance that he will be with them always, to the very end of the age. The disciples are to baptize the converts in the name of the Father, and of the Son, and of the Holy Spirit. Baptism is a public declaration of dying with Christ and rising with him from death to life and glory. Without the resurrection, there is no gospel. The Great Commission is the heartbeat of the mission of Jesus. Christ sending his disciples out on mission was a demonstration of cross-cultural evangelism, and the encounter with the Samaritan woman was a cultural break through.

Biblical Examples of Making Disciples of Societal Plans (John 4:9-19, NIV)

The cross-cultural barrier was broken by Jesus to show how Christians should live together in harmony. Christ met with a Samaritan woman at the well in John 4:9, NIV, and they conversed on two fundamental topics: the "living water" that Jesus gives (John 4:7-18, NIV) and the worship required by God (John 4:19-26, NIV).

With these topics, he broke the barriers in two ways. First, Jesus broke down cultural barriers by speaking with a woman, which was against the Jewish law. The Jews had no dealings with the Samaritans nor with women. Samaritan women, like Gentiles, were considered in continual state of ritual uncleanness. The women were regarded as second-class citizens who had nothing to do with religious/theological discussions;

religious/theological discussion was for men only. Ultimately, according to Jewish rules, Jesus being alone and speaking to a woman at the well broke the rules.

Second, Jesus broke down barriers by speaking to a Samaritan. The Jews had no communion with the Samaritans, would not ask anything from the Samaritans, would not drink from the same jar, nor even sit down with them for meals from the same vessels. Separation between the Jews and Samaritans included no religious and no commercial connection. There was extensive hatred between the two nations. An ethnic gulf between the Jews and the Samaritans existed for centuries. Adam Clarke points out,

> The deadly hatred that subsisted between these two nations is known to all. The Jews cursed them and believed them to be accursed. Their most merciful wish to the Samaritans was that they might not have no part in the resurrection; or, in other words, that they might be annihilated.[9]

The hostility between the Jews and the Samaritans was engraved with hatred and segregation. There was no relationship between them whatsoever. Jesus broke down that barrier by talking with them and walking through their land.

Third, Jesus overcame barriers based on Jewish customs, and his model can be applied to any society in regard to HIV/AIDS positive people. The person with HIV/AIDS experiences stigmatization, isolation, and scorn from society; however, Jesus shows how the Christian response to HIV/AIDS victims can be used to break down cultural barriers. With compassion and love, Christ restored the Samaritan woman and gave her the fountain of the "living water." The text reveals the life of the Samaritan woman and the reason she was socially ostracized in her village. Jesus' example in the text can be extended to those living with HIV/AIDS who are being ostracized from society.

---

[9] Adam Clarke, *The Bethany Parallel Commentary on the New Testament* (Minneapolis: Bethany, 1983), 523.

Restoration of the Outcasts (Luke 17:12-19, NIV)

Jesus not only broke down the social barriers that divided the Jews and the Samaritans, but he also restored those who were ostracized because of diseases, such as leprosy. In Luke 17:12-19, NIV, Jesus confronted lepers who also experienced isolation from society because of the disease they experienced.

Jesus restored ten lepers who were isolated because of their disease (Luke 17:12-19). Bock writes,

> They dare not come near him because of their condition. Ten lepers intend to speak with him, but they cannot approach him because of their despised disease (Lev 13:45-46; Num 5:2-3), so they call to him from a distance. Perhaps the closest cultural equivalent to first-century attitudes about leprosy would be current attitudes about AIDS.[10]

The ten lepers presented their request by calling Jesus "Master" because they had heard of his authority and power to heal the sick. They asked Jesus for his mercy and compassion. Jesus' response was to let them go to the priests to be examined according to the law (Lev 13:19; 14:1-11; Mark 1:44, NIV). Priests were certified to examine the condition of lepers to see or if they were cleansed from the disease. The ten lepers departed as a group and on their way they were healed. Bock writes, "As a result of the healing, these men could resume a normal life—no small cause for thanksgiving and continued in faith."[11]

---

[10] Darrell L. Bock, *Luke*, Baker Exegetical Commentary on the New Testament, vol. 2 (Grand Rapids: Baker, 1996), 1400.

[11] Ibid., 1402.

Christian Service through Love and Care (Luke 10:27-30, NIV)

Jesus demonstrated how Christians should response to HIV/AIDS victims by loving and caring for them. Jesus taught a parable about a Good Samaritan who responded to the immediate need. In the same way, Christians must respond to HIV/AIDS positive people with love and care.

The story of the Good Samaritan is a good teaching lesson for Christians across the globe because it unveils the "law of love," i.e., love needs to be demonstrated not talked about only. The passage beautifully reveals the relationship between God and man and between man and man. Bock writes, "The lawyer answers the question about receiving life in the future in concrete terms of love and devotion, not in an abstract sense. Such love is not marked by the presence of great feeling but is objectively manifested in considerate responsiveness."[12] Bock expresses the kind of love that can be applied by Christians to respond to people living with HIV: "At the heart of the entering the future life is a relationship of devotion, a devotion that places God at the center of one's spiritual life and responds to others in love. . . . Heart, soul, strength, and mind-the whole person-contribute to this response."[13] The parable of the Good Samaritan teaches Christians to love and care for those living with HIV/AIDS.

Bock points out, "The elements of a person described by the four terms depict the emotion, consciousness, drive, and intelligence or cognitive abilities. But there is not compartmentalization of response; the entire person responds."[14] One's devotion to God is expressed by devotion to fellow human beings. Devotion to God and love for others are inseparable. No one can love God and not love other human beings. John reiterates what Luke says, "Anyone who claims to be in the light but hates a brother or sister is still in the darkness. Anyone who loves their brother and sister lives in the light, and there is nothing in them to make them stumble" (1 John 2:9-10, NIV). John also mentions the

---

[12] Bock, *Luke*, 1024.
[13] Ibid., 1025.
[14] Ibid.

kind of love that should be demonstrated by Christians in response to Christian service: "Everyone who loves has been born of God and knows God. Whoever does not love does not know God because God is love" (1 John 4:7b-9, NIV).

The Church Connecting People to God and to Each Other (Acts 4:32-35, NIV)

The Good Samaritan's story teaches Christians to love, care, and help those in need. The early church demonstrated loving and caring for one another in the household of God. HIV/AIDS victims sometimes lack social and spiritual support even from the church. In Acts 4:32-35, NIV, the early church demonstrates how to manage, love, and care for one another.

The early church is a good example of Christian response to the needs of the church members and Christian service. Acts 4:32-35, NIV, says,

> All the believers were one in heart and mind. No one claimed that any of his possessions was his own, but they shared everything they had. With great power, the apostles continued to testify to the resurrection of the Lord Jesus, and much grace was upon them all. There were no needy persons among them. For from time to time those who owned lands sold them brought the money from their sales and put it at the apostles' feet, and it was distributed to anyone as he had need.

The early church displays an active, loving, caring church with a vision. Polhill asserts, "Together they characterized the community life as marked by four things: their unity in mind and heart (v. 32a), their sharing of their possessions (v. 32b), the power and witness of the apostles (v. 33a), and the grace of God, which rested upon them (v.

33b)."[15] The early church was unified and had a loving devotion to the things of the Lord and for Christian service. The passage depicts how Christians in the church should respond to the call to serve.

Conclusion

The biblical and theological support for a teaching series for a Christian response to HIV/AIDS positive people is a call to all. It is imperative to offer a God-honoring way to relate to God's image-bearers who have HIV/AIDS that can be taught to Christians and to all the nations. This section exegetes the meaning of image-bearers and the fall from Genesis 1:26-28, KJV, and Genesis 3:1-16, KJV. The redemptive plan after the fall is an amazing grace that God demonstrated with love of his own people through his one and only Son, Jesus Christ, wrapped in John 3:16 and the Great Commission (Matt 28:18-20, KJV), in which Jesus sends out His disciples to go and make disciples of all nations. Christ crossed social boundaries to meet with the Samaritan woman to show and give her the living water (John 4:9-19, KJV). Similarly, a Christian response is not limited to social and geographical boundaries but extends beyond. A Christian response to HIV/AIDS victims must be through love, compassion, and care, just as Christ demonstrated.

——— THEORETICAL SUPPORT FOR A TEACHING PLAN ———

Theoretical support for a teaching plan for a Christian response to HIV/AIDS is vital to people living with HIV/AIDS. Facts must be established about the origins and treatment of HIV/AIDS, as well as the church's interventions in support of this endeavor. Medical issues and non-issues related to HIV/AIDS must be discussed in order to get to the best solution for a Christian response to the disease. Cultural myths that have been attached to the infection and treatment of HIV/

---

[15] John B. Polhill, *Acts*, The New American Commentary, vol. 26 (Nashville: Broadman, 1992), 151.

AIDS by the society must be examined and corrected in order to have a vibrant impact on discipleship of those with HIV/AIDS.

Origins of HIV/AIDS: Medical Issues

Scientists do not know how the AIDS virus came into existence and where it first appeared in human history. Lyn Robert Frumkin and John Martin Leonard assert,

> An AIDS-like virus causing Simian Acquired Immunodeficiency Syndrome in monkeys has been isolated. A different retrovirus related to HIV has been isolated recently from wild Africa has found cases of unexplained opportunistic infections in patients as early as 1975, that today would meet the current CDC definition of AIDS. It seems likely that the current epidemic may have first occurred somewhere in Central Africa in the mid-1970s.[16]

However, the claim cannot be proven. Some scientists speculate that AIDS first appeared in America among homosexuals:

> In mid-1981, usual opportunistic infections began to occur in homosexuals and users of intravenous drugs in United States. The infections proved to be uniformly fatal and unprecedented in severity in these previously healthy individuals. This apparently new condition was named the Acquired Immunodeficiency Syndrome, or AIDS.[17]

Modern scientists still pursue research to determine the exact origins of HIV/AIDS. Even without an answer to the question of origin, the

---

[16] Lyn Robert Frumkin and John Martin Leonard, *Questions & Answers on AIDS* (Oradell, NJ: Medical Economics, 1987), 12.

[17] Ibid., 1.

impact that the disease has is of great concern because it has created a gulf in families, churches, communities and the whole nation.

There is no treatment to eradicate HIV/AIDS in the body, but some drugs have been discovered that diminish the replication of the virus in the body. Frumkin and Leonard write,

> HIV/AIDS is a chronic disease caused by the human immune deficiency virus (HIV). Acquired immune deficiency syndrome (AIDS) is a disease of the human immune system, which is caused by the immune deficiency virus (HIV).The conditions progressively, reduces the effectiveness of the immune system and leaves individuals prone to many types of diseases.[18]

Medical treatments, including anti-viral drugs and technology that prevent new infections, have been applied to those living with HIV/AIDS. However, when the virus destroys the infected person's immune system, the person is prone to various other diseases. Shepherd and Smith expound,

> The virus is matter which borders by definition between living and nonliving material. They are actually replicable protein matter, which exists in a parasitic sense and can survive only as long as their hosts exist. HIV belongs to a class known as retroviruses because its reproduction process involves the virus using its reverse transcriptase enzyme to replicate its RNA into DNA molecules.[19]

AIDS requires medical treatment, but the available drugs do not treat the disease. Instead, they prevent the disease from multiplying in the cells and leave the victim with a weak immunity and they become

---

[18] Ibid., 13.

[19] Shepherd Smith and Anita Moreland Smith, "Christians in the Age of AIDS," 2, accessed May 2, 2012, http://www.allbookstores.com/Christians-Age-AIDS-Shepherd-Smith.

susceptible to all kinds of diseases, making life-threatening even those diseases that are normally not life-threatening. The drugs are scarce, especially to those in impoverished communities; hence, HIV/AIDS victims die sooner than necessary.

Non-Issues Related to HIV/AIDS

Over thirty years after the discovery of HIV/AIDS, it has become one of the most devastating diseases in human history. Because of a lack of human rights especially, for children and women, the spread of the disease is exacerbated. HIV/AIDS spreads faster in communities where there is social, legal and economic injustice, which creates large disparity between the rich and the poor in any society. HIV/AIDS and poverty open up the environment to spread the epidemic. As cities, churches, and communities grow rapidly, HIV/AIDS infections also spread at an alarming rate. Smith and Smith reports,

> Despite years of HIV/AIDS education programs in Zimbabwe, there are still misunderstandings about the disease, its' genesis, and its effects on the body. HIV/AIDS increased with poverty in the last decade, as those infected with the disease engaged in prostitution.[20]

The spread of HIV/AIDS is exacerbated by a lack of effective educational programs that are designed to inform, educate, and prevent new HIV/AIDS infections. The HIV/AIDS education programs do not apply effectively to the lifestyles of impoverished people groups. The programs are usually aimed at the elite and educated, leaving out the majority of people who are poor and uneducated.

The relationship between HIV/AIDS and human rights is wrapped in three fundamentals: First is vulnerability. In a society, where there is a large social gap between certain groups of people, there is a high risk to poor people to contract HIV/AIDS. The poor hardly understand

---

[20] Ibid., 4.

and realize their social, political, civil, economic and cultural rights. Women and girls are highly vulnerable to HIV/AIDS infections. Second is stigma. Across the social spectrum, HIV/AIDS positive people are discriminated against. As a result, those who have HIV/AIDS avoid contacting local social and health services because they are afraid of discrimination. The HIV/AIDS stigma has escalated infections and prevention of the disease. HIV/AIDS positive people miss available information, education, and counseling benefits. Third is effective response. When human rights are violated and not respected, strategic plans to address HIV/AIDS is hampered and derailed. Prostitutes, homosexuals, drug users, and sex workers avoid such health services. If there are open and supportive programs available to people living with HIV/AIDS, they are more than willing to have HIV/AIDS testing.

Stress, depression, suicides, and abuse of women and children remain the top HIV/AIDS predicaments. HIV/AIDS effects families and communities. Because the psyche of a human being can be affected by circumstances, stress and depression are often the result.

Cultural Myths That Impact Discipleship to Those with HIV/AIDS

Despite a high level of awareness, HIV/AIDS remains highly stigmatized. People living with HIV/AIDS are often perceived as bad people with bad behavior, hence the rise of discrimination. Many people are afraid to be tested because of fear of being socially alienated and discriminated against. Some social taboos may be oppressive to women and these taboos are compounded by patriarchal and conservative systems that have been in place for thousands of years. In parts of the societies, there is myth that says if an HIV/AIDS positive man has sex with a young girl who is a virgin, the virus will vanish from his body system and he becomes HIV/AIDS negative. The myth is heralded by witch doctors who are paid to tell such myths. As a result, older men who are HIV/AIDS positive are abusing many children (girls).

Another myth says HIV/AIDS is a man-made disease designed by Westerners to eradicate certain human beings, especially black people.

The myth claims that white people cannot be infected by HIV/AIDS and that having sex with white people can cure the disease. As a result, HIV/AIDS has spread rapidly with tourists from the west who are lured to have sex with HIV/AIDS positive blacks who believe they will be healed. The myth extends to Albinos, who are thought to be immune from HIV/AIDS because of their DNA, therefore HIV/AIDS positive people have sex with Albinos hoping to get cured.

These myths are baseless; HIV/AIDS does not discriminate and can infect anyone, regardless of color, ethnicity, or race. All races are susceptible to HIV/AIDS. Such mythology deters and hampers the impact of discipleship to those with HIV/AIDS. Myths, even though scientifically untrue, have impact. In writing about African religions, John Mbiti contends, "A myth is a means of explaining some actual or imaginary reality which is not adequately understood and cannot be explained through normal description. Myths do not have to be taken literally, since they are not synonymous with facts."[21] Mbiti reiterates the fact that myths are not equal to truth or reality.

Culturally Contextualized Learner's Needs

HIV/AIDS has decimated family ties, values, resources, relationships, and hopes for the future. Land explains,

> Families with few resources and multiple problems are faced with overwhelming stress upon diagnosis of HIV. Such a diagnosis may overwhelm an already vulnerable family structure and result in a parent's relapse into drug use, abandonment by a partner/spouse, and/or emotional chaos or paralysis leading to the breakdown or dissolution of the family unit.[22]

---

[21] John S. Mbiti, *Introduction to African Religion*, 2nd ed. (London: Heinemann International, 1991), 82.

[22] Helen Land, *A Complete Guide to Psychosocial Intervention* (Milwaukee: Family Service America, 1992), 154.

In Africa in general, women are the victims of abandonment and abuse. The reason the rate of HIV/AIDS infections for women in Africa is rising higher than men is that women are treated as inferiors socially, economically, and legally due to traditional and cultural trends. Musa Wenkosi Dube asserts,

> Women and young girls are more often than not denied the right to property ownership, decision-making and education in patriarchal societies. They become dependent to their husbands, lovers, brothers, uncles or fathers, and are unable to fend for themselves. They have no control over their bodies and therefore are unable to insist on safer sex. . . . Violence in the home, fueled by acceptable gender inequalities, often leave many women afraid to call for abstinence in relationships.[23]

Men tend to dominate women's sexuality (including young girls) in Africa which puts them at high risk. Many women are raped or coerced into sexual situations. Violence against women is rampant in Africa because of culture. In developing a teaching plan, special attention must be given to women and girls so that they can play a part in combating HIV/AIDS.

Conclusion

Theoretical support for a teaching plan as a Christian response to HIV/AIDS positive people requires knowledge of both medicine and myth. Although a cure has been found for HIV/AIDS, anti-viral drugs can help to reduce the replication of the HIV/AIDS virus in the body of the infected person. The teaching plan requires knowledge of available medicine and how it can be applied by medical professionals to HIV/AIDS patients. The knowledge of myths must be understood in the

---

[23] Musa Wenkosi Dube, *The HIV & AIDS Bible* (Chicago: University of Chicago Press, 2008), 103.

context of African society so that they can be dispelled, especially myths about the treatment or cure of people infected by HIV/AIDS disease. A contextualized teaching plan requires knowledge of both medicine and myth in order to have a great impact on evangelism and discipleship of those with HIV/AIDS.

The next section is an overview of the teaching plan that will be conducted to various Christian leaders within the church who have a passion and are ready to be trained to respond to people living with HIV/AIDS. The teaching plan focuses on an exegetical idea, pedagogical idea, and lesson aims—cognitive, affective, and behavioral.

AN OVERVIEW OF THE TEACHING PLAN

Target Group

The target group for this teaching series is Christian leaders of International Christian Baptist Church and any organization that may find the teaching plan valuable. The group met on Saturdays from 12:00 p.m. to 4:30 p.m. for twelve weeks. The group consisted of twenty-five church leaders who were excited about evangelism, discipleship, and gospel transformation. The group was mixed in educational and profession backgrounds. The participants were spiritually mature. The group consisted of both young and senior adults ranging from 21 to 72 years old. Some of the group members had vast work and life experience to share some insight with younger group members. The group was excited to learn and apply the things they learned about a Christian response to HIV/AIDS.

Teaching Focus

Exegetical idea (big ideas). The redemptive plan and the grace God demonstrated through His Son, Jesus Christ, to redeem God's image-bearers in turn calls for a Christian response to HIV/AIDS positive people. Christians should reach out to them with love, compassion, and care. The Scriptures show God's salvation through repentance and belief in His Son, Jesus Christ, and the obedient response in living and sharing the gospel to all nations.

Pedagogical idea (teaching ideas). There is a God-honoring way to relate to God's image-bearers who have HIV/AIDS in order for them to feel loved and cared for within the church and the community.

Lesson AIM (S)

Cognitive (head). The Christian leaders learned that responding to HIV/AIDS is a Christian duty commanded by Christ in the Great Commission (Matt 28:18-20, NIV). They learned how to relate to HIV/AIDS positive people as God's image-bearers in a God honoring way. They also learned that the God-honoring way to respond can be taught to other Christians.

Affective (heart). The Christian leaders reflected on the love, compassion, and supreme sacrifice that Christ gave. They also reflected on their commitment to Christ and learned that Christians should sacrifice their lives in order to serve people living with HIV/AIDS.

Behavioral (hands). Christian leaders engaged emotionally and physically with HIV/AIDS persons.

Teaching Methods

Seminars. Seminars were divided into twelve sessions for 4.5 hours each Saturday.

Cognitive methods. HIV/AIDS video clips, and pictures of those who are living with AIDS were shown. The video clips and photos stimulated the class into thinking critically. Short skits were also used by the participants to demonstrate how HIV/AIDS infections can be prevented. In addition, stories and short games stimulated excitement of students to get involved.

Affective methods. The students were engaged in activities that allowed them to be emotionally engaged and feel the reality of people living with HIV/AIDS in order to change the students' attitudes and take, action to prevent stigmatization and segregation. The students gave their testimonies; demonstrated case studies, had discussions, and role-played.

Behavioral methods. The students were engaged in activities that changed their behaviors and encouraged them to develop new and pleasant behaviors to help those living with HIV/AIDS. Progress charts, mission trips, and support groups helped the students get involved and put what they have learned into practice.

Discussion. After each lecture, there was discussion about the topic so that students could come to conclusions and plan for actions.

Strategic plan. The strategic plan is the class's plans for action as a Christian response to HIV/AIDS positive people.

Application. The application answers how the class plans to apply what they learned and put it into practice as a Christian response to HIV/AIDS positive people.

Evaluation

The evaluation is a tool used to assess and measure the success of the teaching plan. The teaching plan was evaluated on the successful outcome of teaching new content, and the participants' attitudes and behaviors.

The content. The method used for the teaching plan was evaluated by the participants to see if they benefited from it.

The attitudes. The participants' attitudes were measured by pre-seminar and post-seminar surveys. If a comparison between the pre-seminary and post-seminar surveys indicated a change of attitudes about HIV/AIDS positive people, the teaching plan method was deemed successful.

The behaviors. If there is behavioral change of the Christian leaders to intentionally engage HIV/AIDS victims in a more intentional way, the teaching plan and the methods used were deemed successful.

For effective and efficient teaching, the four important segments need to be employed which are Hook, Book, Look and Book.

Conclusion

An overview of the teaching plan gives a glimpse of the outline that started with the target group of Christian leaders from International Fellowship Baptist or any organization. The teaching focus gave insight into the exegetical and pedagogical ideas in teaching plan. The lesson aims highlight cognitive, affective, and behavioral change needed for action in responding to HIV/AIDS. The four important segments of teaching are Hook, Book, Look and Took, which call for productive actions after one discovers the importance of the subject matter. The evaluation assessed the success of the training and the areas of improvements.

───────── IMPLEMENTATION PLAN ─────────

The implementation of the teaching plan occurred over sixteen weeks. In the twelve weeks of seminars, every participant was required to be punctual and well-organized, and to participate. The pre-survey and post-survey were vital to the twelve weeks' seminars to determine the change of attitudes and behaviors toward HIV/AIDS positive people. There is a godly response, biblical support for teaching the response, and theoretical support for teaching that response. The twelve seminars included the following:

The Twelve-Week Seminars

Week 1: Session 1, God's Image-bearers (Gen 1:26-28)
Week 2: Session 2, the Fall (Gen 3:1-16)
Week 3: Session 3, God's Redemption Plan for Humanity (John 3:16)
Week 4: Session 4, Great Commission (Matt 28:18-20)

CONCLUSION

The thesis addressed the Christian response to HIV/AIDS positive people. In a Christian response to HIV/AIDS, there is a God-honoring way to relate to God's image-bearers who have HIV/AIDS and that way can be taught to Christians and other people interested. God's commands and examples in the theological section support the need for this thesis. The fall of man and redemption through Christ Jesus inaugurated new birth to all believers and ushered in the Great Commission, calling all people to repentance. The Christian response to people living with HIV/AIDS is to share the gospel with them, to love them, to have compassion, to disciple, and to connect them to God and the church.

Medical facts and mythical fallacies needed to be addressed in forming a response to HIV/AIDS. The origin of HIV/AIDS and the medical facts and false implications about the possible cure are widespread and needed to be corrected. Depression, stress, and suicide related to HIV/AIDS were addressed in the thesis in forming a response to HIV/AIDS. The mythological beliefs of HIV/AIDS cure through having sex with young girls, albinos, and other races needed to be addressed and corrected in forming a response to HIV/AIDS.

The teaching plan was designed to address these issues with Christian leaders who, in turn, would teach other Christians to respond to HIV/AIDS. Implementation of this plan helped Christian leaders to respond in a God-honoring way to a disease that is rapidly depopulating societies. Consequently, those leaders would teach others to impact the whole of Africa and beyond.

Chapter 2 discusses the *imago Dei* exegetically, the fall and its effects, in terms of the meaning of the fall and the restoration through the death and the resurrection of Christ Jesus. The chapter points to Christ as the perfect image-bearer who came to perfect image-bearers. God's creation of man in His own image and likeness is the center of discussion in chapter 2. The chapter explores the fundamental essence of God's grace and mercy in reconciling sinners to Himself through the death of His Son, Jesus Christ.

— 2 —

THE SIGNIFICANCE OF THE *IMAGO DEI*

INTRODUCTION

The church is the bride of Christ and Christ is the bridegroom. The church represents Christ on earth and is the body of Christ with all its diversity. The church continues the ministry of Jesus Christ to preach, teach, and disciple all those who confess Christ as Lord and Savior. The church has the responsibility to embrace everyone who comes to the church seeking the mercy of God, salvation, healing, and love, and who wants to be part of the body of Christ, regardless of nationality, creed, color, ethnicity and conditions. The church has an obligation to embrace and treat every human being with dignity, love, and mutual respect because they are created in the image of God. This chapter discusses the church's responsibility to treat all human beings as image-bearers (*imago Dei*), regardless of being considered outcasts in society.

The disobedience of the fall resulted in the redemption promise by an image-bearer to image-bearers. Jesus came as a perfect image-bearer to perfect other image-bearers. The disciples share the love of God in the world to all image-bearers as demonstrated by Jesus Christ. The Scripture reveals the need for the disciples to love, embrace, and care for those who are considered to be outcasts in the society. The Great Commission (Matt 28:18-20, KJV) compelled the disciples to preach and make disciples of all nations. The commission includes modern disciples continuing the legacy of making disciples in the diaspora and passing on the faith. In that one charge, the unity of the church has been solidified so that the evangelization of the entire globe will be realized.

——————————— CREATION ———————————

Created in the Image and Likeness of God (Gen 1:26, KJV)

God created all things by his command; however, when God made man, as the crown of his handiwork, there was a dialogue within the Godhead. For God to create man at the end of all creation was an honor and favor. Before man was created, God completely filled the earth with vegetation and animals, a provision for man's survival. God created man with wisdom, unlike any created animals before him. The verse brings in the divine revelation of the Trinity. When God was creating, He said, "Let there be . . ." but when man was made, God made a consultation: "Let us make man in Our own *image*, according to Our *likeness*." In creating the universe, vegetation and animals, God used authority and command, but it was with affection that he created man. The three persons of the Trinity consulted and concurred to make man. Mathews asserts,

> The creation account shows an ascending order of significance with human life as the final, thus pinnacle, creative acts, this is the only one preceded by divine deliberation ("Let us make" in v. 26). This expression replaces the impersonal words spoken in the previous creation acts, (e.g. "Let there be," "Let the earth").[24]

Mathews drives the point that human life alone is special in the sight of God because man was created in the image of God and has a special place in creation.

---

[24] Kenneth A. Mathews, *Genesis 1-11:26*, The New American Commentary, vol. 1A (Nashville: Broadman & Holman, 1996), 160.

Man was made in God's image and after his likeness. These two words express the same thing about *imago Dei*. When verse 26 is examined closer, the interpretation of plural pronouns "let us," "our image," and our "likeness" draw attention to the identity of the Creator. Mathews continues,

> Regarding the verb "make," we have already observed at 1:1 that the verbs "made" (*asa*) and "created" (*bara*) are in parallel both structurally and semantically in 2.4a, b. Here the parallel between v.26 ("Let us make") and v.27 ("So God created") indicates that they are virtual synonyms.[25]

The dialogue within the Godhead displays divine honor in creating human life. Gordon J. Wenham explains, "It refers to the 'fullness of attributes and powers conceived as united within the Godhead."[26] One would concur with the suggestion that it is the plural of fullness.

Wenham presents five views about the "image" and "likeness" in verse 26 that need to be analyzed biblically and theologically. The first view he presents sees "image" and "likeness" as distinctive:

> According to traditional Christian exegesis (from Irenaeus, *ca*, 180 A.D.), the image and the likeness are two distinct aspects of ma's nature. The image refers to the natural qualities in man (reason, personality, etc) that make him resemble God, while the likeness refers to the supernatural graces e.g., ethical, that make the redeemed godlike.[27]

"The image of God" is found four times in the Old Testament, Genesis 1:26, 27; 5:3, and 9:6. In Genesis 5:3, KJV, the text says

---

[25] Ibid.

[26] Gordon J. Wenham, *Genesis 1-15*, Word Biblical Commentary, vol. 1 (Waco, TX: Word, 1987), 28.

[27] Ibid., 29.

Adam fathered a son "after his image." Victor Hamilton argues, "The Hebrew word for "image" is *selem,* which the LXX normally renders by *eikon* (icon). . . . Here *image* would be something conveying the idea of emptiness, unreality, insubstantiality."[28] This view may not express the original meaning of the text although, theologically, it may sound correct. The second view, by Wenham, suggests, "The image refers to the mental and spiritual faculties that man shares with his creator. The image of God resides in man's reason, personality, free-will, self-consciousness, or intelligence."[29] Scholars continue to refine the meaning of the terms "image" and "likeness" and they continue to find specific clues in Genesis to understand how the image was interpreted.

The third view, described by Wenham, contends,

> The image consists of a physical resemblance, i.e. man looks like God. The physical image is the most frequency word, *selem.* Genesis 5:3 Adam is said to have fathered Seth "after his image," which most naturally refers to similar appearance of father and son.[30]

The fact that both Old and New Testaments stress that God is Spirit and He is invisible diminishes this view. However, the view should not be dismissed outright because Jesus said, "If you had known Me, you would have known My Father also; and from now on you know Him and have seen Him" (John 14:7, NKJV). Jesus answered Philip's question about showing them the Father. There remains debate about whether Jesus was referring to his physical appearance or his spirituality that resembled his Father.

Wenham states the fourth view as "The image makes man God's representative on earth. That man is made in the divine image and is thus God's representative on earth was a common oriental view of the king. Both Egyptian and Assyrian texts describe the king as the image

---

[28] Victor P. Hamilton, *The Book of Genesis: Chapters 1-17,* The New International on the Old Testament (Grand Rapids: William B. Eerdmans, 1990), 134.
[29] Wenham, *Genesis 1-15,* 30.
[30] Wenham, *Genesis 1-15,* 30.

of God."[31] Wenham highlights that man was given power and authority to rule and subdue the rest of creation; man was created a little lower than the angels, crowned with glory, and made to rule the handiwork of God. John Sailhamer reiterates that man was created with a special place in the creation:

> Throughout the previous narrative each creature is made "according to its own kind" (*l'minah*). But the account of the creation of humankind specifically notes that the man and the woman were not made "according to their own kind." Rather, they were made "in (God's) image" (*b'salmnu*). They are not merely like themselves, they are also like God; they share a likeness to their Creator.[32]

The author of Genesis puts emphasis on the creation of man—that they were created "male and female" (v. 27), which is a contrast with other creation stories in which gender is not mentioned.

Wenham's fifth view asserts, "The image is a capacity to relate to God. Man's divine image means that God can enter into personal relationships with him, speak to him, and make covenants with him."[33] Wenham points out that this view is supported by Karl Barth and Westerman: "Barth holds that the phrase 'in our image' modifies the verb 'let us make,' not the noun 'man.' There is a special kind of creative activity involved in making man that puts man in a unique relationship with his creator and hence able to respond to him."[34] The fifth view suggests that God created man in order to relate with him in a personal way. Out of the five views, the last view seems favorable because humans are the only created beings that can relate, talk, and make covenants with God. Man is a special creature that God intended to communicate with directly.

---

[31] Ibid., 31.

[32] John H. Sailhamer, *Genesis*, in vol. 1 of *The Expositor's Bible Commentary*, ed. Frank E. Gaebelein, Walter C. Kaiser and Richard Hess (Grand Rapids: Zondervan, 2008), 69.

[33] Wenham, *Genesis 1-15*, 31.

[34] Ibid.

Created to Make Others Who Have God's Image and Likeness (Gen 1:28, NKJV)

God blessed Adam and Eve and said, "Be fruitful and multiply' fill the earth and subdue it; have dominion over the fish of the sea, over the birds of the air, and over every living thing that moves on the earth." God gave the human family the privilege and responsibility of taking care of all creation. As sin entered the earth, it negatively affected the prosperity of the earth and all living things in it.

God gave Adam and Eve two assignments: procreation and dominion. To all animals, God gave power to reproduce themselves. In Mesopotamia and Canaan, creation motifs were linked to fertility rites, and Genesis 1:28, NKJV, puts that concept to rest. Reproduction is a God-given blessing and gift, which is not dependent on rites devoted to gods or idols. The purpose of God giving man a mandate to multiply and fill the earth was so that man would rule over the animals. God gave Adam and Eve a divine purpose for marriage: the procreation of children. It is God's purpose, will, and desire to bless his people with children and fill the earth. The blessing of God to be "fruitful" and "fill" the earth is the source from which human race emanate. John Calvin writes,

> But here Moses would simply declare that Adam with his wife was formed for the production of offspring, in order that men might replenish the earth. God could have himself indeed have covered the earth with a multitude of men; but it was his will that we should precede from one fountain, in order that our desire of mutual concord might be the greater, and that each might the more freely embrace the other as his own flesh.[35]

In the same vein, it is in God's power, within his will and purpose, to allow some to be fruitful and others be barren. This barrenness might

---

[35] John Calvin, *Commentary on Genesis, Commentaries on the First Book of Moses*, vol. 1 (Grand Rapids: Baker, 1996), 97.

be the result of a medical condition, biological complication, or simply the will of the Lord. God is Sovereign, and He does what He wants for special purposes. Russel Reno alludes,

> The power of 'begetting" serves as the engine of history in Genesis and in scripture as a whole. The generations are the streams of forward movement. Procreation gives us a future. . . . As the command "be fruitful and multiply" emphasizes, we are physically equipped to live in the image of God, because we possess the potential for new life.[36]

To have a child is to have a future because children perpetuate the family tree and become the next generation. The future of the law is carried on to obedient children, as illustrated in Deuteronomy 6:6-7, KJV. The angels were not made "male" and "female," for they were not to procreate and propagate their kind (Luke 20:34-36, KJV), but man was mandated to do so to continue the race. Reno explains, "The *imago Dei* is found in our giving birth to and nurturing children whom we cannot finally control. Children become independent agents who eventually supersede us."[37] Reno further discusses that procreation is not only biological reproduction, but procreation is spiritual potential. Spiritual births of the children are through witnessing and evangelization of the entire globe. New life in Christ is procreation in the truest sense.

Created to Rule as God's Representatives (Gen 1:28)

Man was created as God's representative on earth. Man is the crown of God's creation and he has a special mandate bestowed on him by God. He is accountable for everything on earth in the sky, the land, the waters, the animals, and to other human beings, to be his "brother's keeper."

---

[36] Russell R. Reno, *Genesis,* Brazos Theological Commentary on the Bible (Grand Rapids: Brazos, 2010), 56.
[37] Ibid., 57.

God mandated man to rule and subdue over all the living creatures of the sky, and of the land and of the water. Air and water pollution, land deforestation, and the killing of creatures to use their flesh as food was not mandated. It was after the flood that domination in the consumption of animals was extended to man (Gen 9:3). Hamilton propounds,

> Of the two verbs, *rada*, "exercise dominion," and *kaba*, "subdue," the later connotes more force. Thus, it refers to subjecting someone to slavery (2 Chr 28:10; Neh 5:5; Jer 34:11, 16), to physical abuse. . . . All these references suggest violence or display of force. For reasons already indicated, it appears unlikely that we need to transfer the nuance of force and dictatorship into the use of *kabas* in Gen 1:28.[38]

Humankind should treat animals with dignity and take care of the environment, including water, air, and the land.

All creation was to be subdued by man as God's representative and God gave the humankind power to rule: "This is a place in which God has set man to be the servant of his providence in the government of the creatures, and, as it were, the intelligence of the of this orb, to be the receiver of God's bounty, which other creatures live upon."[39] Fruitfulness is dependent on God the creator. The Hebrew tradition was that love for earth was sacred and human righteousness was connected with the welfare of the earth. "A righteous man regardeth the life of his beast: ..." (Prov 12:10a; 27:23; Deut 25:4, KJV).

---

[38] Hamilton, *The Book of Genesis*, 139.
[39] Ibid., 140.

The Disobedience of the Fall (Gen 3:1-7, NKJV)

There was a mutual relationship and harmony between God and man before sin entered the human race through Satan's deception. God commanded, "Of every tree the garden you may freely eat; but of the tree of the knowledge of good and evil you shall not eat, for in the day that you eat of it you shall surely die" (Gen 2:16-17, NKJV). God alone knows what is good for man. In order for man to enjoy the "good," man must trust and obey God in every word that he spoke/speaks. When man disobeys God, he decides for himself what is good and bad. The serpent, the perpetrator of deceit in the garden, is mentioned as more, "crafty" (*'arum*) than any of the creatures. Sailhamer writes,

> The description of serpent as "crafty" is in keeping with the fact there are several features of this story that suggest that the author wanted to draw a relationship between the fall and man's quest for wisdom. Man's disobedience is not so much depicted as an act of great wickedness of a great transgression as much as it is an act of folly. He had all the "good" he would needed, but he wanted more-he wanted to be like God.[40]

The forbidden tree is the knowledge of "good" and "evil." In the passage are two main subjects—God versus Satan—and Eve chooses to obey Satan rather than God.

The serpent speaks two times and that is enough to offset trust and obedience between man and his Creator. "Then the serpent said to the woman, you will not surely die. For God knows that in the day you eat of it your eyes will be opened, and you will be like God, knowing good and evil" (Gen 3:4-5, NKJV). The serpent implied that God

---

[40] John H. Sailhamer, *Genesis*, in vol. 2 of *The Expositor's Bible Commentary*, ed. Frank E. Gaebelein (Grand Rapids: Zondervan, 1990), 50.

was keeping his divine knowledge to himself. The serpent questioned God's command to man and challenged his credibility as the Creator. Both Adam and Eve participated in disobeying God's command not to eat the fruit from the tree of the knowledge of good and evil. Torre asserts, "The serpent is the first creature in the biblical text to objectify God, talking about God rather than talking to God or with God. Keeping God from the discussion, it is able to tempt the woman with a forbidden fruit."[41] The serpent was tempting Eve to disobey what God had commanded them to eat and not to eat in the garden. The serpent instilled doubt in Eve's mind and heart. When she disobediently ate the fruit, alienation between man and God occurred. Eve shared the fruit with Adam and immediately they discovered they were naked. The desire for food, the lust of eyes, and the quest for wisdom apart from God, compelled Eve to disobey God. "So, when the woman saw the tree was good for food, that it was pleasant to the eyes, and desirable to make one wise, she took of the fruit and ate" (Gen 3:6, NKJV).

The serpent purposely exaggerated and distorted God's prohibition to man that God was jealous, self-protective, and that he was cruel and an oppressor. Eve's response to the serpent is also exaggerated and contains distorted statements. Adam was given the instructions and the command before Eve was created. He distorted and exaggerated what God had said. She could not have understood clearly what God had commanded Adam; however, there is no excuse for sin. She added, "You shall not eat it, nor shall touch it" (v. 3). She also does not mention God's statement, "You shall surely die" (Gen 2:17b, NKJV). Instead she says, "Or you will die." The serpent capitalizes on her oversight. John Walton asserts,

> First, a technical study of the syntax shows that the serpent knows enough to deny the precise penalty as God worded it. God's statement in 2:17, "You shall be doomed to death" is identified as an absolute infinitive

---

[41] Miguel De La Torre, *Genesis, Belief: A Theological Commentary on the Bible* (Louisville: Westminster John Knox, 2011), 68.

coupled with the finite verb of the same root. To negate this sort of syntactical construction, the negative particle is placed between the two verbs forms, in effect negating the finite verb. . . . Instead, the negative particle precedes both verb forms, thus negating the absolute infinity. This construction occurs only two other times in the Old Testament (Ps. 49:8; Amos 9:8). Since the absolute infinitive serves in these cases to indicate the inevitability of the action, the negation of the infinitive absolute is a negation of the inevitability.[42]

The serpent paints the picture of God's statements, but they are a misrepresentation and distortion of God's statement to Adam. Both Adam and Eve were responsible for their sin against God.

The apostle John warns of adding or subtracting to the Word of God:

For I testify to everyone who hears the words of the prophecy of this book: If anyone adds to these things, God will add to him the plagues that are written in this book; and if anyone takes away from the words of the book of this prophecy, God shall take away his part from the Book of Life. (Rev 22:18-19)

The warning tells that no one should ever distort or exaggerate the Word of God, either adding or subtracting from it; Eve and Adam included.

After eating the fruit, their eyes were opened immediately, and they were conscious that they were naked (v. 7). Their nakedness gave them shame. The knowledge they thought they would acquire after eating the forbidden fruit was not the knowledge they realized. Instead, they realized nakedness. They were ashamed of each other and God.

Adam and Eve's quest for wisdom, to be like God, was the pride

---

[42] John H. Walton, *Genesis*, The NIV Application Commentary (Grand Rapids: Zondervan, 2001), 204-5.

of sin. When Adam and Eve saw that they were naked, they covered themselves with fig leaves, which was a temporary remedy to their problem. In providential grace and love, God sought them out and found them. He clothed them with animal skin. Man desired to be like God. They sought wisdom but found vanity and toil.

Adam was crowned as the head and had been given the responsibility to assign names to all the animals (Gen 2:20, NKJV) and his wife (Gen 2:23, NKJV). They had sinned by disobeying God and were immediately experiencing the consequences of that sin. They began to put themselves in charge and covered their shame and nakedness with withering leaves that do not last. Hamilton contends,

> The verb sewed (*tapar*) occurs only more three times in the OT (Job 16:15; Eccl 3:7; Ezek 13:18). In Job 16:15 and Ezek 13:18 it means "to wear" (sackcloth, arm bands, i.e., some kind of clothing that is next to skin). Why the man and woman chose fig leaves is not clear.[43]

Some scholars believe that fig trees were the largest trees in Palestine, which is why the couple chose its leaves to cover themselves. However, they could not cover their shame and sin of disobedience.

The Consequences of the Fall—The Image Is Marred: Pain, Suffering, Death (Gen 3:16-19, NKJV)

The consequences of the fall have gross effects on all humankind, the animals of the forest, birds of the air, the ocean creatures, and the whole universe. Sin distorted what God initially intended man to be and the image is deformed and twisted from its original form. Life changes for the worse; there is pain, suffering, and death because of sin. God pronounces his judgment for disobedience to man.

In verse 16, God pronounces judgment on Adam and Eve and on the serpent: "To the woman He said, 'I will greatly multiply your sorrow

---

[43] Hamilton, *The Book of Genesis*, 191.

and your conception: In pain you shall bring forth children; Your desire shall be for your husband, and he will rule over you." The woman is given two judgments: one related to child bearing and the other being overruled by her husband. First, God would increase pain and toil: she would give birth in agony. God created man and woman to enjoy the sanctity of good relationship in marriage, which was to be a source of blessing, but now was distorted by sin. When God created the woman, he did not talk about the pain the woman was going to experience. After the fall, God pronounces that he would increase the pain; "increase" meaning to add on something that already exists. Walton expounds,

> The noun translated "pain" in the first line is a word used only two other times in the Old Testament (Gen 3:17; 5:29). Nouns from the same root refer to pain, agony, hardship, worry, nuisance, and anxiety. The verb root occurs in a wide range of stems with a semantic range that primarily expresses grief and worry.[44]

The verbal root includes physical pain, which embodies psychological anguish. The pain and suffering she will go through is the consequence of her actions in submitting to the temptation and deceit of Satan.

The woman will experience anxiety in the process of conception to birth. Pain and suffering of a woman starts with the anxiety of her ability to conceive and bear a child. If she conceives, she is bombarded by the anxiety of whether or not she will bear a healthy baby. She has worries throughout her pregnancy, including physical discomfort and her survival and the baby's survival at delivery. These are all strenuous pains and sufferings bestowed on the woman for her disobedience.

Second, her "desire" will be for her husband and he will rule over her. According to Hamilton, in Genesis, "The Hebrew word for *urge* or '*desire*' occurs only here and in Genesis 4:7, NKJV. In the Canticles references it has a decidedly romantic and positive nuance, describing

---

[44] Walton, *Genesis*, 227.

a feeling of mutual attraction between two lovers."[45] According to Walton, "desire" extends outside Genesis and

> occurs only two other times in the Old Testament (Gen 4:7; Song 7:10). This means that the synchronic database is slim, but that does not mean that it can be ignored. Gen 4:7 occurs not only in the same general context but also features similar circumstances on the syntax and discourse level.[46]

The woman's desire is to be dependent to the husband for fulfillment in her maternal instinct. The woman's desire is to have children and to be a mother. Relations between human beings suffer. McKeown states, "While human beings still enjoy some of the benefits of blessing such as the ability to procreate, they must contend with the new situation where the world and its inhabitants are out in harmony with the Creator."[47] Their lives changes forever and the relationship between themselves and God are marred.

Verses 17-19 say, "Then to Adam He said, 'Because you have heeded the voice of your wife and have eaten from the tree of which I commanded, saying, 'you shall not eat it': "Cursed is the ground for your sake; in toil you shall eat of it all the days of your life." The man's punishment for disobedience was expulsion from the Garden into hard labor for his survival. Robert Sacks writes,

> The world outside the Garden is still that dry, hard land which required rain and a man to toil. After man had been formed he appeared to be too noble to be placed in such a position. God tried to rectify the situation by

---

[45] Hamilton, *The Book of Genesis*, 201.

[46] Walton, *Genesis*, 228.

[47] James McKeown, *Genesis,* Two Horizons Old Testament Commentary (Grand Rapids: William B. Eerdmans, 2008), 37.

planting the Garden, but Man was incapable of leading such a life.[48]

Man could not freely eat of the produce provided by the Creator because the good and fertile land was cursed. God had given Adam and Eve freedom to eat from any tree of the garden except one. Man was to work and toil for his food for survival and to provide for his family. "Cursed is the ground because of you; through painful toil you will eat of it all the days of your life."

God's judgment matches the sin in the fact that the man's sin was that he ate (3:6, 12). Hamilton points out,

> In response to man's trespass of eating, God speaks no less than five times of eating in his word to man (vv. 17 [3 times], 18, 19). Thus, the penalty on the man parallels the penalty on the serpent. To both God says a word about their eating. Similarly, God's word to the man parallels his word to the woman, for in the experiences of both there will be *pain* (Heb. *Issabon*). For her the pain will be connected with childbearing, and for him the pain will be connected with food. *Issabon* and the verb *asab* obviously refer to physical pain, but they also embrace the concept of anguish.[49]

God did not pass judgment on man as an external punishment that required physical labor and planning for his survival, unlike the woman who received internal pain and suffering from within her body. The woman would have pain and suffer as a mother and a wife and the male as a breadwinner and family provider. The judgment of man and woman are not temporary, but permanent situations until they return to the ground from where they came.

Sin began in heaven with the pride of Lucifer, not on earth. Adam

---

[48] Robert D. Sacks, *A Commentary on the Book of Genesis,* Ancient Near Eastern Texts and Studies, vol. 6 (Lewiston, NY: Edwin Mellen, 1990), 35.
[49] Hamilton, *The Book of Genesis,* 202.

and Eve succumbed to temptation and the results were disastrous. Judgment from God came in three parts: a war between the woman and the serpent, the woe on the woman on childbearing and as mother and wife, and work for man to toil and labor for food in the field to provide for the family. John Philips states, "But the curse went beyond the serpent to Satan himself. God asked no questions of him. In that declaration of war Adam and Eve heard the gospel message for the very first time."[50]

"In the sweat of your face you shall eat bread Till you return to the ground, for out of it you were taken; for dust you are, and to dust shall return" (Gen 3:19, NKJV). Death was judgment, which was devastating to Adam and Eve, for when they were created, they were to live forever. Adam was created from the dust, the earth, and because of the sin of disobedience, he would die and return to earth from which he came. Returning to the earth was a separation between God and man. John Gill explains,

> His body was composed of the dust . . . and should be reduced to that again by death, which is not an annihilation of man but a bringing him back to his original' which shows what a frail creature man is, what little reason he has to be proud of himself, when he reflects from whence he came and whither he must go.[51]

Death was both physical and spiritual, and God's relationship with man was different because of Adam's disobedience. Physical death brought about pain, suffering, murder, war, hunger, disease, and hate as the result of sin through Adam and Eve. Spiritual separation from God means there is no longer direct communication with the Creator. There is no spiritual connection between God and man because sin separated them.

---

[50] John Phillips, *Exploring Genesis, John Phillips Commentary Series* (Chicago: Moody, 1980), 61.

[51] John Gill, *An Exposition of First Book of Moses Called Genesis* (Lebanon, MO: Particular Baptist, 2010), 67.

Adam and Eve became the parents of a race of sinners throughout the ages. Rice asserts, "The taint is in the blood. The curse is on every cell of their bodies. The curse will be on every child they shall bring forth and every descendent down through the millenniums."[52] Rice reiterates that every fabric of the human body is sinful and deserves death. Sin not only corrupted and distorted the human body, but it altered his spiritual composition as well. Sin brought disastrous effects to human physical and spiritual composition. Adam and Eve died both physically and spiritually. "Therefore, just as through one man, sin entered the world, and death through sin, and thus death spread to all men, because all sinned" (Rom 5:12, NKJV).

The Consequences of the Fall—The Image Is Marred: Separation from God (Gen 3:22-24, NKJV)

Sin separated man from God and the relationship between God and man was broken. The sin of rebellion and disobedience made God angry, and the mutual relationship that previously existed between God and man was tainted. "Then the Lord God said, 'Behold, the man has become like one of Us, to know good and evil. And now, lest he put out his hand and take also of the tree of life, and eat, and live forever" (v. 22, NKJV). The Lord expelled him out of the Garden of Eden to till the ground from which he was taken. John Marks contends,

> Man has stepped outside the state of dependence, he has refused obedience and willed to make himself independent. The guiding principle of his life is no longer obedience but his autonomous knowing and willing, and thus he has really ceased to understand himself as creature.[53]

---

[52] John R. Rice, *Genesis: "In the Beginning . . ."* (Murfreesboro, TN: Sword of the Lord, 1975), 143.

[53] Gerhard Von Rad, *Genesis: A Commentary*, trans. John H. Marks (Philadelphia: Westminster, 1961), 94.

Man was destined to death after the sin of disobedience. However, even though man was driven out of the garden and prevented from approaching the tree of life, God still loves and shows mercy toward him.

Herbert Leupold draws attention, "Whereas in v.8-21, NKJV, we had the substance of what God spoke to man in mercy and in judgment, we have in v. 22 NKJV, the persons of the Holy Trinity in divine counsel among themselves."[54] Leupold writes,

> But since, to the best of our knowledge, no tree of itself can possess such virtues, it seems best again with Luther to assume that this remarkable power was characteristic of the tree not by its inherent natural qualities but by virtue of the power of the Word of God, who was pleased to ordain that such should be the effect of partaking of the fruit of this tree. For man in his fallen and sadly altered state the acquisition of the quality of imperishability for this sin-torn and sin-defaced body would have a grievous calamity.[55]

It is imperative to understand that had man eaten of the tree of life, Christ's work to restore fallen man would not have been feasible, bearing in mind that man would be like God and live forever. Although death was the ultimate result of the fall, God in His sovereignty prepared the redemption of fallen man through Christ Jesus.

God had compassion and mercy for man. He wanted to save His creatures from the power of sin. Phillips writes,

> God moved in to rescue the wretched creatures who had fallen so low. He did so first in *grace* (3:20-21), for salvation is always through grace. Adam had discovered that the fig leaves of his own self-effort would not do in the presence of God. . . . There, in Eden, in paradise

---

[54] Herbert C. Leupold, *Exposition of Genesis Chapters 1-19,* Christian Classics Ethereal (Grand Rapids: Baker, 1950), 180.
[55] Ibid., 181.

itself, blood was shed for the very first time. . . . It was the first dramatic illustration of the ultimate cost of Calvary, of the horror and dreadfulness of sin. Sin is a radical disease, and it calls for a radical cure.[56]

Adam and Eve could have seen the gruesome death of the slaughtered animal for their covering instead of their fig leaves covering, signifying the first test of the gruesome death of Christ for the shedding of blood for sinners. Phillips reiterates, "To rescue the fallen pair God acted not only in grace, but He acted also in government"[57]

It was in God's mercy and grace that he drove them out of the Garden of Eden and prevented them from eating of the tree of life. God showed unbelievable love to fallen man. God made sure that Adam and Eve would not eat of the tree of life by placing guards, the Cherubim, at the east of the Garden of Eden, and a flaming sword that turned every way, to guard the way to the tree of life. Phillips explains,

> If Adam and Eve, in their fallen condition, had eaten of that tree, they would have lived forever in their sins. They would have become like the fallen angels, incapable of death and forever locked into the guilt and penalty of their sins. It would have been impossible to renew to repentance. God in His government did not allow that to happen.[58]

One would agree with Phillips in his analogy about the fallen angels who are not capable of repenting and being redeemed. God did not want human beings to have the state of fallen angels.

In God's command, the Cherubim, in contrast to the fallen angels, were God's representatives. The Cherubim are God's angels whom God uses in His government to accomplish His purpose in the world (Ps 18:10, NKV). Leupold writes,

---

[56] Phillips, *Exploring Genesis*, 63.
[57] Ibid.
[58] Phillips, *Exploring Genesis*, 64.

The root from which the word may be derived would suggest that the word as such means "a brilliant appearance" (*glanzerscheinung*). How these marvelous beings appeared was well remembered by the Israelites at least, for they seemed to require no further description when they were told to make two cherubim upon the mercy seat of the ark of the covenant and otherwise to use the figures of the cherubim for ornament purposes, (Ex 25:18; 26:1).[59]

The separation of God and man because of the sin of disobedience was disastrous, yet God did not give up on His creatures. The fundamental question to be posed is, are there some traits of *imago Dei* in God's fallen creatures? The next section explores and discusses whether or not the image of God is still in man.

The Image and Likeness Remains (Gen 5:1-3, NKJV)

Scriptures reveal that the image and likeness of God remained in man even after the fall. As a royal representative of God, man is still the only crown of life of God's creation. Genealogy is the perpetuation of the original:

> This is the book of genealogy of Adam. In the day that God created man, He made him in the likeness of God. He created them male and female and blessed them and called them Mankind in the day they were created. And Adam lived one hundred and thirty years, and begot a son in his likeness, after his image, and named him Seth, (Gen 5:1-3).[60]

Being the original created being in the image and likeness of God and representing God, God commanded Adam to procreate with Eve for his off springs resembling him. Hamilton propounds,

---

[59] Leupold, *Exposition of Genesis*, 184.
[60] Leupold, *Exposition of Genesis*, 184.

Vv. 1b-2 are introductory superscription that describes the cause of the effects detailed in the following verses. That Adam reproduces himself through Seth, and Seth through Enoch, etc., demonstrates that God's blessing has become effective. They are not only created in by God but blessed by God. Such blessing is manifested in multiplication. It is appropriate that the creation of man be prefaced to Adam's descendants through Seth rather than through Cain.[61]

The contrast of God creating Adam, and then Adam reproducing himself in his son, Seth, is an illustration of a divine and natural phenomenon. It is interesting to see God perpetuate His image and likeness in man. Hamilton continues, "Furthermore, the reference to Gen. 1 at the start of this chapter permits a contrast between a divine creative act and human creative acts. In a sense Adam and his posterity are doing what God did. He created, and they are procreating."[62] After creating them male and female, God blessed them and charged them to multiply and fill the earth. The divine image and likeness is transmitted from generation to generation with the genealogy of the firstborn son. In tracing the account of human sin and death, one can also see the continuing effects of sin and God's promise of procreation and blessing from the beginning. God preserves Adam's seeds through procreation as He promised and blessed him.

Based on God's promise and blessing to "...Be fruitful and multiply; fill the earth and subdue it..." (Gen 1:26-28, NKJV), Adam and Eve fulfill that promise. Mathews explains,

> It shows the evolution and universality of human wickedness, which deserves God's angry reprisal (6:1-8), but again, despite this, the hope that rests in God's favor toward Noah (5:29; 6:8-9). . . . Although these two lines of descents have superficial similarities, they

---

[61] Hamilton, *The Book of Genesis*, 255.
[62] Ibid.

also present a stark dissimilarity. There is no linkage between Cain and Adam in the formal genealogy (4:17-24). The connection is derived only from the earlier narrative at 4:1. In the Sethite listing the setting of creation is preeminent (5:1b-3) for the purpose of cohesion between Noah and first things (Adam). Cain's connections with creation, on the other hand have been discounted-he is disowned!-and the rite of passage for blessing will be through Abel's successor, Seth.[63]

The omission of Cain in the genealogy is to look for hope and blessing in the future through the family line of Seth instead of Cain. Cain was the first born, but he did not inherit any right to the promise because of his actions—Seth is awarded that right. The image of God still exists in man; however, it is no longer a perfect image, but an imperfect image and likeness. McKeown asserts,

If 5:1-3 is read without considering its context, the reader will almost certainly conclude that human beings are no longer in the image of God. Thus, whereas the Creator makes Adam in his own image-the image of God— Adam had a son in *his* own image. As God created man, in his own perfect image, so now, sinful Adam has a son in his own imperfect image.[64]

Adam passes his own image to his younger son, Seth, for Cain was rejected in favor of Seth. The image in man makes him superior to all the animals, even after the flood (Gen 9:6, NKJV). This proves that the image of God was not withdrawn, even if man sinned and fell short of the glory of God.

The image and likeness of God in man makes man still the crown of life of all the creation on earth. In his imperfect and sinful state, man still has dominion and rules God's creation. McKeown explains,

[63] Mathews, *Genesis 1-11:26*, 296.
[64] McKeown, *Genesis*, 45.

"Now, in contrast, the effect of God's image in people and of his continued blessing on the human race is in focus through the progeny of Seth."[65] According to verse 3, Seth has his father's image and likeness. There is no biblical support to say that God withdrew His image and likeness from man when he disobeyed. However, there is evidence of imperfection in man because of sin (Rom 3:23, NKJV). Cain's family genealogy purports humans moving away from God while Seth's family genealogy aligns toward restoration and building the broken relationship with God. Reno writes,

> Seth is enrolled with Adam in the project of physical survival that brings death as its future. . . . Thus, the genealogy flowing from Adam gives us a picture of a fresh but failed effort to escape the gravitational force of the first sin. Even as the genealogy begins anew with Seth, he and his descendants slowly but inevitably trace a declining arc toward the target of death.[66]

The image and likeness of God in Adam is passed on to Seth from generation to generation. Adam's descendants embody sinful imperfections, and the result is death.

However, God planned for redemption and restoration through God-man, Jesus Christ, the Savior of the world. God's grace and love for created beings was so powerful that He gave His only Son to die on the cross for sins. The next section discusses the redemption of sinful man to salvation through Christ Jesus.

---

[65] Ibid., 46.
[66] Reno, *Genesis*, 112.

Redemption Promised by an Image-Bearer
for Image-Bearers (Gen 3:15, NKJV)

"And I will put enmity between you and the woman; and between your seed and her seed; he shall strike your head, and you shall bruise his heel" (Gen 3:15, NKJV). The judgment of God to the woman and her seed versus the serpent and its seed is very dramatic. The two parties involved would be enemies. The seed of the woman would bruise the head of the serpent and the seed of the serpent would bruise his heel. This was prophetic for the virgin birth. In general, the ancient world believed that only man could deposit the seed and a woman would be only an incubator until she gave birth. The prophetic message was the virgin birth of Jesus Christ (Luke 1:1-36, NKJV). Walton expounds on the seed:

> The word "seed" is a collective noun that typically takes singular pronouns standing in its place. Therefore, when the text says *he* will crush your head, grammar cannot determine whether this is a reference to the corporate seed or one representative from among the descendants. The use of the singular "you" ("your head" and "you will strike") has sometimes been considered an indication that this must refer to Satan because the serpent does not continue to exist through the generations.[67]

The conflict is between the seeds of the two parties involved. The war between them is formidable and required one of them to win. In the history of the church, it has been believed that the seed of the woman is Christ and has defeated Satan at Calvary. Walton suggests,

> The verbs "crush" and "strike" are now properly identified as belonging to the same root, *swp*. We must therefore

---

[67] Walton, *Genesis*, 226.

conclude that the actions performed are comparable. For this reason, the translation of the verb should be fairly generic so as to be suitable to both a strike to the head and a strike to the heel.[68]

The strike on the head causes more damage than a strike on the heel. The strike on the head destroys the head and kills the seed of the serpent. The strike on the heel does not cause lethal damage. Leupold observes,

> This is too obvious to require lengthy defense; for when man steps on a serpent's head, a crushing result; but when the serpent strikes while the contest is on, only a sting on the heel or a bruising result. But at the same time a crushed head spells utter defeat. A bruised heel may be nursed till healed.[69]

The seed of the woman (Christ) crushed Satan entirely and destroyed him (1 Cor 15:55-57, NKJV). Continual bitter conflict between humans and the evil in the world and hostility between the serpent and the man still exist. Whenever man and serpent meet, there is always conflict that involves life and death. There is always struggle between man and serpent. The exegesis of the text finds a messianic prophecy—a reference to a final victory of the seed of the woman (*protevangelium*).

Satan possessed the serpent as a tool for sin. The serpent became the symbol of sin for all mankind. However, the victory is guaranteed to the seed of the woman and the defeat of the serpent. One born of a woman would win the victory. Isaiah 53 designates the coming Messiah. Leupold writes,

> It should be clearly observed that his gracious promise is the opening of the sentence or doom that God pronounces. Even on the first pages of the Bible we are

[68] Ibid.
[69] Leupold, *Exposition of Genesis*, 166.

shown the face of God 'merciful and gracious, slow to anger and abundant in goodness and truth' (Exod 34:6). He delights in showing mercy. . . . Grace, provocative of faith, precedes the sentence.[70]

The early church and the modern church believe the Messianic prophecy portrayed in (Gen 3:15, NKJV). The text depicts the coming Messiah born of a virgin, Mary. Leupold puts beautifully how Christ completed the task of crushing the head of the Satin:

> A significant New Testament, yet however, looms up very prominently and serves as the same purpose; after Christ's public ministry is officially inaugurated by the His baptism, He encounters the devil in a temptation, even as the first parents encountered him. This, first of all, confirms the fact that the first tempter was the devil, but it more distinctly displays the first crushing defeat that the seed of the woman administered to His opponent. On the cross this victory was sealed and brought to its perfect conclusion. The cry, "It is finished," marked the successful completion of the task.[71]

The seed of the woman finally put an end to both the power of sin and Satan. All Christians are under the protection and guidance of Christ who conquered Satan and death that was brought by the sin of rebellion. The image-bearer brought salvation to image-bearers through His sacrifice and death on the cross. The Second Adam brought life unlike the first Adam who brought death. The next section discusses the redemption through Christ Jesus who came as the perfect image-bearer.

Jesus came as the perfect image-bearer (2 Cor 4:4; Col 1:15; Heb 1:1-4, NKJV). "Whose minds the god of this age has blinded, who do not believe, lest the light of the gospel of the glory of Christ, who is the

---

[70] Leupold, *Exposition of Genesis*, 168.
[71] Ibid., 170.

image of God, should shine on them" (2 Cor 4:4, NKJV). Satan will continue to perpetuate evil influence until Christ returns to establish God's kingdom in the full (Gal 1:4). Those who deny and do not believe in the power of the gospel cannot appreciate or fully understand the claims of the gospel, unless God through the Holy Spirit and the gospel enlightens them (John 3:3, NKJV). He is the prince of darkness and the ruler of the darkness of this world. He blinds, deceives, enslaves, and darkens hearts of the multitude of people in the world. He sways many to disbelieve in the gospel of Christ. Colin Kruse asserts,

> *The god of this age* refers to Satan, who is permitted to exercise a limited rule in the present age (John 12:31), a rule that will be terminated although with the coming of the new age at Christ's return. In the meantime, he is active in blinding the minds of unbelievers to the truth of the gospel.[72]

Paul spoke about the veil over the Jewish contemporaries who could not understand their own Scriptures as well as other unbelievers. Satan also veils believers to deceive and misguides them in order to hinder God's work. Paul mentions that Christians may hear the gospel but not appreciate its truth because Satan blinds them. Kruse explains,

> Paul says that the gospel is the glory of Christ, *who is the image of God.* There may be an allusion here to the creation of human kind in Genesis 1:26 ('Then God said, "Let us make mankind in our image, in our likeness'), especially in the light of the fact that Paul does speak of Christ as the 'last Adam,' comparing (and contrasting) him with the 'first Adam' (I Cor 15:45-49; Rom 5:12-19). . . . For Paul, Christ the is the image of God after the fashion of Adam as far as is his humanity

---

[72] Colin G. Kruse, *2 Corinthians*, Tyndale New Testament Commentaries, vol. 8, rev. ed. (Downers Grove, IL: IVP, 2015), 140.

is concerned and after the fashion of Wisdom as far as his transcendence is concerned.[73]

Christ is the image of the invisible God because He is co-essential with the Father. Christ is the image of God who reveals the Father. Christ demonstrates the power and wisdom of God and his grace and mercy for the salvation of all sinners. The gospel reveals the glory of Christ who is the image of God. The glory of Christ is His divine and human excellence centered in His personality. Charles Hodge writes,

> Christ, in his divine nature or as *Logos*, is declared to be "the radiance" of the Father's "glory" (Heb 1:3), to be in the form of God and equal with God (Philippians 2:6, and perhaps also Colossians 1:15). But here is the incarnate *Logos*, the exalted Son of God clothed in our nature, who is declared to be the image of God, because "all the fullness of the Deity lives" in him "in bodily form" (Colossians2.9).[74]

Christ is the image of God incarnate and the perverted image in Adam is replaced by Christ's image, the perfect image. Christ is the full representation of God and the expression of the nature of God, making God visible in Him.

Colossians 1:15, NKJV, says, "He is the image of the invisible God, the firstborn over all creation." Christ is the divine nature in His works of creation and providence. He is in Himself the image of God; the true representation of God. Daniel Wilson contends,

> The word image is used in two senses in Scripture, as it is still in our ordinary language. It sometimes means any resemblance, slight or not, of another person or thing, according to the nature of the subject spoken of.

---

[73] Ibid., 142.

[74] Charles Hodge, *2 Corinthians*, The Crossway Classic Commentaries (Wheaton, IL: Crossway, 2015), 74.

So, Adam was created "in the image of God," not as fully resembling God, but bearing some faint likeness to him in 'righteousness and true holiness.[75]

Christ is consubstantial with the Father and has the same nature, qualities, perfections, power, and essence as the Father. Wilson explains that Christ possesses the glory of God: "It teaches us that Christ the uncreated Word and Wisdom of the Father, is his perfect image and resemblance, his exact counterpart; possessing all his glory, attributes, perfection, and powers, as the natural and only-begotten Son of God."[76] Christ is the image of the invisible God. The image of God in Christ denotes His perfect quality with the respect of His substance, power, and eternality.

The Son is the Father's image in all things. Moule reiterates Christ's image of God: "Not that the reference of the 'Image' here is directly or primarily to our Lord's Body of the Incarnation, but to His being, in all ages and spheres of created existence, the Manifester of the Father to created intelligences."[77] Christ is the first born of all creation as the image of God. He is the reflection of the Father and radiates the attributes of the Trinity. The deflected image of God in man that was marred in the fall is restored in Christ. He is the new Adam in perfect image, reflecting the glory of God in his divine nature.

In Hebrews 1:1-4, NKJV, is written,

> God, who at various times and in various ways spoke in time past to the fathers by the prophets, has in these last days spoken to us by His Son, whom He has appointed heir of all things, through whom also He made the worlds; who being the brightness of His glory and

---

[75] Daniel Wilson, *Expository on Colossians, Verse-by-Verse Bible Commentary* (New York: Bible House, 1859), 73.

[76] Ibid., 74.

[77] Handley Carr Moule, *Studies in Colossians and Philemon* (Grand Rapids: Kregel, 1977), 77.

express image of His person, and upholding all things by the power.

John Phillips points out,

In the person of the Lord Jesus, God found a perfect vehicle of expression. He simply translated Deity into humanity, or, as John puts it, "The Word was made flesh" (John 1:14). . . . Moreover, Christ is "the express image" of God. The phrase "express image" refers to something "engraved" or "impressed" as, for instance, a coin or seal that bears line for line all the features of the instrument making it.[78]

The incarnation was an expression of God to reach out to a fallen human kind in order to save it. The expression of God's image is engraved in Jesus.

The author of Hebrews elucidates how God's expression of His image was revealed in Christ. Phillips expounds on the expression of God's image in Christ: "The lines of Deity have been reproduced in Jesus' humanity; so, to find out God is like we need only look at Jesus. We can take the lines of Christ's personality and draw those lines on out into infinity and obtain a perfect concept of God."[79] Christ is God manifest and God in substance. He is the reproduction of God; He is the image of the invisible God. John MaCarthy writes, "The word 'image' here is *eikon*, from which we get *icon*. *Eikon* means a precise copy, an exact reproduction, as in a fine sculpture or portrait. 'For in Him dwells all the fullness of the Godhead bodily,' (Col 2:9,)."[80] God has made known the glory of His character through Christ His Son.

James Haldane expounds, "By contemplating in Him the glory of

---

[78] John Phillips, *Exploring Hebrews, The John Phillips Commentary Series* (Grand Rapids: Kregel, 1977), 21.

[79] Ibid., 22.

[80] John MacArthur, *Romans1-8, The MacArthur New Testament Commentary Series* (Chicago: Moody, 1983), 16.

the Lord, we are changed into the same image from glory to glory as by the Spirit of the Lord. This is the new creation in Christ Jesus, which is essential to our being His disciples."[81] The image and likeness, which was marred in mankind, was restored and inaugurated in Christ and then it was sealed. Those who believe in Christ are made whole through the work of the Holy Spirit. The shedding of the blood of Christ for the remission of sin was completed in Christ and expiated the anger of God. Christ reconciled mankind to God and He paid the price in full. The new creation infused to all believers is completed and sealed by the Holy Spirit.

Jesus came to perfect other image-bearers (Rom 8:29; 1 Cor 15:49; 2 Cor 3:18; Col 3:10, NKJV). "For whom He foreknew, He also predestined to be conformed to the image of His Son, that He might be the firstborn among many brethren" (Rom 8:29, NKJV). The word predestined (*prohorizo*) occurs six times in the NT (Acts 4:28; Rom 8:29, 30; 1 Cor 2:7; Eph 1:5, NKJV). Theologically, the essence of predestination indicates that God has the plan and the design and has prepared salvation for those called by His name—they are called by God's purpose (*prothesis*). To be predestined is to be conformed to the likeness of His Son. MacArthur asserts,

> Foreknew. Not a reference simply to God's omniscience-that in eternity past He knows who would come to Christ. Rather, it speaks of a predetermined choice to set His love on us and established an intimate relationship-or election. A Greek grammar, called the Granville Sharp rule, equates "predestination" and "foreknowledge."[82]

Predestination is God's foreknowledge of those who are God's own who will be conformed to be like Christ. The security of salvation of

---

[81] James A. Haldane, *Hebrews*, Newport Commentary Series, 2nd ed. (Springfield, MO: Particular Baptist Press, 2002), 13.

[82] John MacArthur, *The MacArthur Bible Commentary* (Nashville: Thomas Nelson, 2005), 1533.

the believers is embedded in Christ and they have already been destined to eternity in Christ. MacArthur highlights,

> Predestined, literally, "to mark out, appoint, or determine beforehand." Those whom God chooses, He destines for His chosen end-that is, likeness to His Son. Ephesians 1:4, 5, 11, conformed to the image of His Son. The goal of God's predestined purpose for His own is that they would be made like Jesus Christ. This is a "prize of the upward call" (Phil. 3:14; Eph.4:13; Phil. 3:20, 21; Col. 1:28).[83]

Paul writes using the past tense as if it has already happened because for him it is already done with absolutely certainty. Price gives an interesting argument, "Christians who have borne-and continue to bear the image of the man of dust shall also bear the image of the man of heaven. This hope has its present counterpart in Paul's conviction that men in Christ already bear this image, though not visible."[84]

Conformity to Christ's image is not from human endeavor but through the sanctification of the Holy Spirit when believers are transformed into His image and likeness. The Holy Spirit perfects the saints into the image of Christ daily and prepares them for the day of the second coming of Christ in glory.

First Corinthians 15:49, NKJV says, "And as we have borne the image of the man of dust, we shall also bear the image heavenly Man." In light of this text, Henry Ironside elaborates on the heavenly man:

> There are also celestial bodies, that is, heavenly bodies, and bodies terrestrial, earthly bodies. Our Lord came into this world and took a terrestrial body, but after having made satisfaction for our sins on the cross, He came forth in resurrection in a celestial body, and in

---

[83] MacArthur, *The MacArthur Bible Commentary*, 1533.

[84] James L. Price and Charles M. Laymon, eds., *Interpreter's One-Volume Commentary on the Bible* (Nashville: Abingdon, 1980), 811.

that body He ascended through the heavens into the very presence of God. . . . His celestial body is the pattern of what ours shall be; we shall have bodies in resurrection that are not subject to the laws that control us now.[85]

The bodies of the saints will be changed from corruptible flesh and blood, into incorruptible glorious and spiritual bodies suitable to the celestial world for eternal inheritance. The bodies of the believers will be similar to Christ's resurrected, glorified physical body. His redeemed people will receive spiritual and imperishable bodies to live with Christ forever.

Second Corinthians 3:18, NKJV, says, "But we all, with unveiled face, beholding as in a mirror the glory of the Lord, are being transformed into the same image from glory to glory, just as by the Spirit of the Lord." The Spirit enables believers to be like Christ. Hodge propounds,

Conformity to Christ's likeness, since it arises from seeing his glory, must, of course, begin here. It is the vision of that glory, although only as in a mirror, that has transforming power. It is the vision of that glory, although only as in a mirror, that this has transforming power.[86]

Hodge points out that the glory of Christ is his divine excellence, hence the believer is enabled to see that Jesus is the Son of God. The believers shall be like Christ because they will see him as is (1 John 3:2, NKJV). The believers shall conform to Christ's likeness. Paul reiterates, "And as we have borne the imagine of the man of dust, we shall also we shall bear the image of the heavenly Man," (1 Cor 15:49, NKJV). The bodies of Christians shall have a transformation that resembles Christ.

---

[85] Henry A. Ironside, *I and 2 Corinthians, An Ironside Expository Commentary* (Grand Rapids: Kregel, 2006), 283.
[86] Hodge, *2 Corinthians*, 67.

This may mean the transformation proceeds from glory (that is, from the glory of Christ as apprehended by us) and results in glory. This explanation is adopted by the Greek Fathers. Or the expression indicates progression from one stag of glory to another. The transformation is carried forward without intermission, from the first scarcely discernible resemblance to full conformity to the likeness of Christ, both in soul and in body.[87]

The principles laid in 3:17 are employed in 3:18, NKJV, with the application of the spiritual transformation of believers.

In expounding 2 Corinthians 3:18, NKJV, Peter Naylor contends,

Further, the intensification of their glory is spiritual, not facial and physical, their inner man "being transformed" into the "likeness" or image (Greek, eikon, whence the English 'icon'/ikon) of Christ. This comes about through the work of the 'Lord, the Spirit' who operates in the hearts of his people.[88]

The text explains that Christians behold the mirrored glory of the Lord, seeing and reflecting God through the image of God, the Lord Jesus Christ. It is important to understand that Paul in the text is expounding the concept that all believers will have the same bodies as Christ. Ralph Martin propounds, "The verb 'being transformed,' suggests a link with Christ, as God's 'image,' who is the prototype for all who belong to him and in whom he is taking shape (Gal 4:19, NKJV)."[89] The believers shall take the form, shape, image and likeness of Christ because they will be with him for eternity. Their glorified

---

[87] Ibid., 68.

[88] Peter Naylor, *A Study Commentary on 2 Corinthians* (Darlington, England: Evangelical, 2002), 164.

[89] Ralph P. Martin, *2 Corinthians*, Word Biblical Commentary, vol. 40, 2nd ed. (Grand Rapids: Zondervan, 2014), 215.

bodies shall be in conformity with that of Christ to live in heaven with God, which will be a glorious day that everyone should wish for.

Colossians 3:10, NKJV, says, "And have put on the new man who is renewed in knowledge according to the image of Him who created him." The believers' position is acceptance in Christ, and they are granted spiritual power and regeneration. Moule writes, "By union with Him his members become repetitions of Him the glorious Archetype. . . . So as to be like God, who created, constituted the new creation as He did the old."[90] The image of God consisted in man's resemblance to the moral attributes of God. Wilson explains,

> But the moral likeness to his all-glorious Maker was the principal part of man's honor. . . . So that knowledge, righteousness, true holiness, and a disposition to delight in all good works, constitute the main parts of the image of God in Adam was created; the dominion over the creature accompanying it.[91]

His restoration back to God is only possible through the sacrifice and mediation of Christ. Wilson puts an emphatic point in saying that the new man resembles, in some faint degree, the perfections of the Creator. He bears his image in his moral attributes as he exhibits a distant resemblance of righteousness, holiness, and beneficence.[92]

The image of putting away old nature and putting on new nature marks the transition from vices to virtues. After the renewal of all the vices in a person, virtues set in through the work of the Holy Spirit, thus renewing the image of God in believers. The new life in a believer begins to shape character, attitude, behavior, and lifestyle. The renewal of the inner being is not merited to any individual because their efforts; good works cannot please God because it is the work of the Holy Spirit. The passive voice shows that the result does not come from man's efforts or works, but the Holy Spirit sanctifies believers to be more like Christ.

---

[90] Moule, *Studies in Colossians & Philemon*, 125

[91] Wilson, *Expository on Colossians*, 295.

[92] Wilson, *Expository on Colossians*, 298.

Christ came to perfect other image-bearers to be more like Him. The believer becomes a new person, old things pass away—all things become new and the believer becomes the creative handiwork of God.

The next section discusses the consummation in which Christ establishes God's kingdom and the final completion of work perfecting image-bearers. Paul expounds on the consummation and Christ establishing God's kingdom forever.

Consummation

Jesus will return to establish God's kingdom completely. The kingdom of God will be established by Christ on His return. Christ inaugurated the kingdom of God in His death and resurrection. Although He is present today among His people, it is not in all his fullness. When He returns to earth at the appointed time, the Lord's righteous rule will be recognized by all creation, including His enemies under His feet (1 Cor 15:27-28, NKJV). When a Pharisee asked Jesus about the coming of the kingdom of God, Jesus answered, "The kingdom of God does not come with observations; nor will they, say 'See here!' or see there!' For indeed, the kingdom of God is within you," (Luke 17:20-21, NKJV). The kingdom of God is partly present and partly future. The kingdom of God is a reality and is available now to overcome Satan and spiritual forces. Consummation is the coming together of everything that marks the completion, fulfillment, and realization of the kingdom of God when Christ returns for the second time.

Jesus' second coming has numerous interpretations in which the church has been divided by beliefs about his kingdom. Keith Bailey points out,

> The Second Coming of Jesus Christ is an article of faith among all who call themselves Christians, but beliefs about the details of His return and the relationship of His return to the kingdom of God divide the church into three major camps: the amillennialists,

the postmillennialists, and the premillenialists. One of the key differences centers on interpretation of the thousand-year period mentioned in Revelation 20.[93]

Amillennialists do not believe in the literal one-thousand-year reign of Christ; instead, they interpret Revelation 20 as the church age at present. The second group is postmillennialists, who believe that when the church engages in aggressive evangelism and there is revival in the church, then the kingdom of God will come, and after one thousand years of Christ's blessings, Christ will return to establish His kingdom and the world will end. The third group is premillennialists, who believe that Christ is coming again, and He will set up the kingdom of God. They believe in the reality of the kingdom literally and that it will take place for the period of one thousand years.

The first coming of Christ brought in moral, social, and spiritual changes, and His second coming for the consummation of the kingdom and judgment of all humankind will be new beginning for everything. Christ's kingdom will be gracious, spiritual, and redemptive. Hodges distinctively points,

> The kingdom of God is to be distinguished from the kingdom of heaven in five aspects: 1. The kingdom of God is universal, including all moral intelligences willingly subject to the will of God, whether angels, the Church, or saints of past or future dispensations, while the kingdom of heaven is Messianic, mediatorial, and Davidic, and has for its object the establishment of the kingdom of God in earth. 2. The kingdom of God is entered only by new birth; the kingdom of heaven, during this age, *is the sphere of profession which may be real or false.* 3. Since the kingdom of heaven is the earthly sphere of the universal kingdom of God, the two have almost all things in common. . . . 4. The kingdom of

---

[93] Keith M. Bailey, *Christ's Coming and His Kingdom* (Harrisburg, PA: Christian Publications, 1981), 7.

comes not with outward show; but is chiefly that which is inward and spiritual; while the kingdom of heaven is organic and is to be manifested in glory on earth. 5. The kingdom of heaven merges into the kingdom of God when Christ, having 'put all enemies under his feet,' shall have delivered up the kingdom to God, even the Father.[94]

The kingdom of God is consummated when Christ returns for the second time to establish God's kingdom. Hodge puts it into perspective with logical analysis. God's kingdom is for born-again Christians, who are the bride of Christ, the church. The qualification for the kingdom of God is the grace of God and redemption through repentance and forgiveness by Christ Jesus. Christians are then transformed into newness through the work of the Holy Spirit who sanctifies the believer into the image and likeness of God. The next section discusses Jesus completing his work of perfecting image-bearers.

Jesus will complete his work of perfecting image-bearers (1 Cor 1:8; Eph. 1:4; Phil 1:9-11; Col 1:22; Rev 20:7-10, NKJV). "Who will also confirm you to the end, that you may be blameless in the day of our Lord Jesus" (1 Cor 1:8, NKJV). Mark Taylor writes,

Paul expands on the thought of the Day of the Lord by affirming, "He will keep you strong to the end." The context, this confirmation is further explained as "blameless," that is, without accusation on the Day of the Lord. Colossians 1:22 provides further insight on Paul's meaning: "But now he has reconciled you by Christ's physical body through death to present you holy in his sight, without blemish and free from accusation."[95]

---

[94] Jesse Wilson Hodges, *Christ's Kingdom and Coming* (Grand Rapids: Wm. B. Eerdmans, 1957), 23.

[95] Mark Taylor, *1 Corinthians*, The New American Commentary, vol. 28 (Nashville: B & H, 2014), 45.

The image-bearers are being sanctified by the Holy Spirit—being perfected until the return of Christ when He will complete the work of perfecting them. Jay Adams asserts,

> In perfect, glorified bodies that are like the risen body of Jesus, we shall be able to appreciate and bask in the glory of God. Once cleansed and perfected, we will be able to approach the God who has always been unapproachable because of our infirmities and our sins. There, made perfectly holy, in perfect bodies, circumstances will be rapidly different.[96]

Adams points out that believers will have perfect bodies, like that of risen Christ with a glorified body.

Paul expounded the concept of a glorified body for all believers as Christ was after His resurrection. Paul then strikes a chord when he says they have been sanctified in Christ Jesus and are called to be holy. In Ephesians, Paul expounds that Christ will perfect image-bearers: "Just as He chose us in Him before the foundation of the world, that we should be holy and without blame before Him in love" (Eph. 1:4, NKJV). Paul discusses the fact that Christ chose His people before the foundation of the world, and in essence, in His sovereignty, grace, and love, Christ perfects and sanctifies His chosen people to be like Him. Andrew Lincoln asserts,

> In Eph. 1:4 holiness, blamelessness, and love are complementary terms. On its negative sides holiness is the absence of moral defect or sin, i.e., blameless, while, on its positive sides, as moral perfection, it displays itself in love which is the fulfillment of God's will. In this reference a theocentric perspective predominates, for a life of holiness, blamelessness, and love has its source in and response to the gracious election of God and is

---

[96] Jay E. Adams, *Hope for the New Millenniums* (Woodruff, SC: Timeless Text, 1994), 15.

lived 'before him,' that is, conscious that God's presence and God's approval are one's ultimate environment.[97]

Lincoln extends the horizon of God's foreknowledge about those He chose before the foundation of the world.

According to Scripture, predestination is God's foreordaining what is going to pass in history. In His divine power, God prepares in advance and chooses beforehand what will take place; He has foreknowledge about the future. Harry Uprichard writes,

> If predestination is God's ordering of destiny, then *election is* God's choosing of persons. . . . The New Testament continues and develops this theme of election as God's means of choosing sinner for salvations. Paul notes the purpose of election, which is with a view to holiness: "to be holy and blameless in his sight." Holiness is that moral purity and apartness of God which he bestows in salvation on the Christian.[98]

The doctrine of election is not dependent on human knowledge, efforts, or power, but is determined by God alone who is sovereign and omniscient. Some churches have over-emphasized or exaggerated the doctrine of election and predestination.

God's foreknowledge about the future is further discussed by Walter Taylor:

> The activity of God in blessing is further detailed by **chose** and **destined**. The verb **chose** is literally the word "elect"; the word **destined** is the Greek word for "foresaw." The electing activity of God is no late breaking development. It occurred before the world was created

---

[97] Andrew T. Lincoln, *Ephesians*, Word Biblical Commentary, vol. 42 (Dallas: Word, 1990), 25.

[98] Harry Uprichard, *A Study Commentary on Ephesians* (Darlington, England: Evangelical, 2004), 34.

and it occurred in him, that is, in Christ. Likewise, in his love, God foresaw (**destined**) through Jesus Christ that the recipients would be God's children.[99]

God chose believers before the foundation of the world. He redeemed Christians and destined them to eternity without blemish.

In Philippians 1:9, NKJV, Paul wrote, "And this I pray, that your love may abound still more and more in knowledge and all discernment..." Todd Still asserts,

> The assembly is to be marked by purity as they await and anticipate the Parousia (on "day of Christ. To be sure, this level of moral excellence requires diligence and vigilance on the part of believers. In the spiritual striving, however, they are to be mindful that the fruit of righteousness they seek is available in and is attainable through Christ.[100]

For Paul, standing right with God, and right living before God reflects Christ's righteousness and God's glory. Paul specifically urges the Philippians to produce the "fruits" of righteousness. Gerald Hawthorne and Ralph Martin write,

> Paul makes it clear, however, that this crop of goodness is not self-generated, nor can it be. For the "fruits" he has in mind is supernatural and is produced through Jesus Christ. . . . God is the ultimate finality of the Christian life, and as such he alone to be honored and praised by all.[101]

The Holy Spirit enables believers to live righteous lives and to

---

[99] Walter F. Taylor, *Ephesians*, Augsburg Commentary on the New Testament (Minneapolis: Augsburg, 1985), 34, emphasis original.

[100] Todd D. Still, *Philippians and Philemon*, Smyth and Helwys Bible Commentary (Macon, GA: Smyth and Helwys, 2011), 34.

[101] Gerald F. Hawthorne and Ralph P. Martin, *Philippians*, Word Biblical Commentary, vol. 43 (Nashville: Nelson Reference and Electronic, 2004),

produce fruits. Christ is perfecting image-bearers and will complete the work when He comes for the second time.

Colossians 1:22, NKJV, complements other texts that have been presented about how Christ will complete the work of perfecting the image-bearers. Robert Wall reiterates,

> Verses 13-14 help us understand what happens at the beginning of our spiritual journey, when we are converted to or confirmed in Christ for our salvation from darkness and death. Verses 15-20 celebrate Christ's current and cosmic lordship over God's creation and new creation, and show why we can be confident, even in the midst of a broken and fallen world. . . . Finally, based on verses 12-23, we are drawn toward the future, we are drawn toward the future, the eternal consequences of our reconciliation with God through Christ.[102]

Christ is in the business of perfecting image-bearers, and the Holy Spirit guides believers to live holy and righteous lives in order to draw others to Christ as they reflect the glory of God. Living a righteous life is the work of the Holy Spirit living in Christians.

Nicholas Wright points out the fundamental reasons why the Colossians should exhibit the fruits of the Holy Spirit:

> Paul now applies verse 20 to the problem of verse 12 and concludes that God *has reconciled you by Christ's physical body through death to present you holy in his sight.* He does not say that God's action in Christ, and the Colossians' acceptance of the gospel, have automatically and instantly made them perfect. Having been given a new life, they must behave in accordance with it.[103]

---

[102] Robert W. Wall, *Colossians and Philemon,* IVP New Testament, Commentary (Downer Groves, IL: IVP, 1993), 82.

[103] Nicholas T. Wright, *Colossians and Philemon*, Tyndale New Testament Commentaries, vol. 1 (Downers Grove, IL: IVP, 1986), 82.

Christ's purpose is to present Christians before God as holy in His sight and without blemish. The language in the quote is in accordance with the Jewish sacrificial ritual, which denoted sacrifice without blemish or defects. God creates a holy people in Christ. Wright continues,

> This he is doing in practice, by refashioning their lives according to the pattern of the perfect life, that of Christ. This he will do in the future, when that work is complete and the church enjoys fully that which at present it awaits in hope. The present process, which begins with patient Christian living and ends with the resurrection itself, will result in Christians being presented without shame or fear before God, as glad subjects before their king.[104]

Christians are being molded in the image and likeness of Christ and being sanctified by the Holy Spirit, and Christ will complete the work of perfecting image-bearers at the proper time.

The book of Revelation contains apocalyptic literature that entails allegories and figures that need accurate interpretations. With special reference to Revelation 20:7-10, NKJV, John writes the book with clarity of his vision from his imprisonment in the island of Patmos: "Now when the thousand years have expired, Satan will be released from his prison" (v. 7). The book of Revelation gives a detailed timeline of symbolic events. Parallel to the book of Revelation is the book of Daniel, which is also apocalyptic in nature, depicting the symbolic events at the end of the age. James Hamilton explains,

> Revelation presents Daniel's seventieth week as taking place between Christ's ascension and his return. At the end of Daniel's seventieth week, Christ comes in judgment and fights the Battle of Armageddon (16:12-16; 17:14; 19:19). At the conclusion of the battle, the beast and the false prophet are thrown into the lack of

---

[104] Wright, *Colossians and Philemon*, 83.

fire (19:20), and Satan will not join the lake of fire until the thousand years (20:20).[105]

From his visions, John writes the events as if he were seeing them happening. For a thousand years, Satan is not thrown into the lake of fire; instead, he is seized and bound and is thrown into Abbys, shut and sealed over him for a thousand years. The believers who remained faithful at the start of a thousand years are raised from the dead and will reign with Christ for a thousand years (Rev. 20:4-6, NKJV).

After a thousand years, Satan is then released and "And will come out to deceive the nations that are at the four corners of the earth Gog, Magog, to gather them for battle; their number is like the sand of the sea" (Rev. 20:8, NKJV). John then writes about Satan being thrown into the lake of fire with false prophets: "And the devil who has deceived them was thrown into the lake of fire and sulfur where the beast and false prophets were, and they were tormented day and night forever and ever" (Rev. 20:10, NKJV). Hamilton asserts, "Amillenialists argue that the battle in (Rev. 20:7-10, NKJV), is another description of the battle in 19:17-21, but the details are simply too different for that to be the case."[106] Satan and the false prophets are neither pardoned nor annihilated. In (Rev. 20:7-10, NKJV), John writes about the final battle at the end of the millennium. John does not tell why Satan is being let loose. Mitchell Reddish writes,

> In a typical apocalyptic understanding, all that happens occurs within the ultimate purposes of God. Even the lease of Satan is John's way of emphasizing the formidable power of evil. Even when it appears that the evil has been contained and is no longer a threat, it has the capacity to rebound and wreak havoc in one's life.[107]

---

[105] James M. Hamilton, *Revelation: The Spirit Speaks to the Churches* (Wheaton, IL: Crossway, 2012), 376.

[106] Hamilton, *Revelation*, 377.

[107] Mitchell G. Reddish, *Revelation*, Smyth and Helwys Bible Commentary (Macon, GA: Smyth and Helwys, 2001), 385.

As John writes, Gog and Magog symbolize those nations that are deceived by Satan and those whom God will destroy. God will be declared the supreme ruler.

According to Reddish, John borrowed the Gog and Magog tradition:

> Whereas in Ezekiel, Gog is a person and Magog is the land over which he rules, in Revelation both Gog and Magog have become the names of evil nations. In Ezekiel, even though Gog has taken on mythical proportions, he is still a localized threat, the foe from the North. In Revelation, Gog and Magog are all-embracing symbols for all the nations or peoples who are in rebellion against God.[108]

God finally defeats Satan and Satan's doom is at the conclusion of the millennium. Lamar Cooper presents three interesting arguments, which are summarized by Paige Patterson:

> Lamar Cooper, in the New American Commentary volume in Ezekiel, chronicles seven possible interpretations of the battle but finds in the end three major possibilities. The first is the Gog and Magog actually refers to the same battle by that name in Revelation 20. The second views the battle as Armageddon at the close of the tribulation period, chronicled at the end of chap. 16. The third view is a combination of the first two, including that this final conflict of history occurs at two different times with an interim period of 1,0000 years.[109]

Gog and Magog represent false prophets who have been deceived by Satan to perpetuate his deception. The devil has deceived many people

---

[108] Ibid., 386.

[109] Paige Patterson, *Revelation*, The New American Commentary, vol. 39 (Nashville: B & H, 2012), 356.

and, together with his false prophets, will be thrown into the lake of fire where they belong, and God will summon them for eternal punishment.

All the enemies of God—Satan, false prophets, and those who chose not to serve God—will be thrown in the lake of fire for eternity. Patterson writes, "Apparently part of what it means to be made in the image of God is to have indestructibility or immortality as part of what it means to be a spiritual being. A choice is to be made as to whether one wishes to be associated with God or to be left his own prowess."[110] It is imperative to understand that, in the New Testament, hell was not originally made for human beings, but it was made for Satan and his angels (Matt 25:41, NKJV). However, the lake of burning fire with sulfur, *Gehenna*, is the place for Satan with his angels and those who reject Christ. The devil and his angels will experience excruciating torment for eternity. Christ will then usher in a new heaven and new earth where the perfected image-bearers will abide with Christ forever. Eternity for the righteous and holy, perfected by Christ, will inherit and live in harmony forever with the Lamb, Christ Jesus.

The *imago Dei* in humanity makes humans unique and different from other animals. God created man in His own image and likeness to display His glory on earth through humanity. After the fall, the image and likeness of God in man were impaired and distorted. However, some imprints of God's image and likeness in man remain because God did not reduce man to the level of animals. God restores His image and likeness in man through His Son, Jesus Christ, the perfect image-bearer. Other image-bearers have been redeemed through the death and the resurrection of Christ. God's image-bearers have been redeemed to proclaim and share God's love. The next chapter lays out a teaching series that will help Christians in Zimbabwe to proclaim and share God's love by living out the Great Commission with people with HIV/AIDS.

---

[110] Ibid., 358.

—3—

THEORETICAL SUPPORT FOR A TEACHING PLAN

―――――――――――― **INTRODUCTION** ――――――――――――

HIV/AIDS disease has had a negative impact on families, churches, and society. The church has an obligation to address and provide support to curb the spread of HIV/AIDS. Therefore, a teaching plan is urgently needed to address the epidemic before the disease drastically depopulates the society. HIV/AIDS not only affects those who are infected, but it affects families, the church and society. Infected persons are always pondering death while also considering those they will leave behind. They develop anger toward those whom they think might have infected them, such as spouses, friends, sexual partners, or parents. They become depressed but, at end, most accept their conditions.

It is in this context that this chapter discusses medical issues and the origins of HIV/AIDS, including transmission, stigma, prevention, and medical consequences. The mythical beliefs about HIV/AIDS, cultural stigma, and cultural impact are also discussed. This chapter concludes with a discussion of a cultural and biblical corrective in which biblical standards are suggested as the solution to decrease the transmission of HIV/AIDS in the midst of church discipleship programs.

Origin of HIV/AIDS

It is imperative to understand how and when AIDS came into existence in order have adequate information and to know how to deal with this complex disease. According to Sam Puckett and Alan Emery,

> the AIDS virus made its first appearance during the 1960s or perhaps earlier in several countries in South Central Africa. The virus is one of a particular class of viruses known as retrovirus. . . . This new form of retrovirus has been named by its various discoveries as "Human T-Lymphotropic Virus Type III" (HTLV-3), "Lymphadenopathy Associated Virus" (LAV) and AIDS Retro Virus (ARV). In 1986 an international science committee gave it the official designation "Human Immuno-deficiency Virus," or "HIV." To the public it is known as "the AIDS virus" and the medical condition it causes is known as "AIDS"— Acquired Immune Deficiency Syndrome.[111]

The AIDS virus is one of the scariest and most feared diseases in human history. HIV/AIDS is an infectious disease caused by the Human Immunodeficiency Virus (HIV).

Betty Moffatt explains,

> Acquired Immune Deficiency syndrome (AIDS) is the result of a defect in the immune system's family ability to resist certain types of infections: those caused by viruses, fungi, parasites, and mycobacteria (tuberculosis-like organism). . . . It means that AIDS is not a disease in itself. The mortality rate from AIDS comes from the

---

[111] Sam B. Puckett and Alan R. Emery, *Managing AIDS in the Workplace* (Reading, MA: Addison, 1988), 1.

body's inability to resist what is known as 'opportunistic infections.[112]

According to Moffatt, the person dies from the failure of the body's immune system to defend against illnesses:

> The living with AIDS description of the medical diagnosis of AIDS as affecting the immune system in ways currently under study and revision by researchers. . . . The term "acquired" is used because people with AIDS are known to have normal immune system function prior to the onset of the syndrome.[113]

Some misconceptions about HIV/AIDS infections make it more feared. Since its discovery, the origin of HIV/AIDS has been a mystery. Although there have been many theories of its origin, these hypotheses cannot be substantiated in record. Scientists do not know how the AIDS virus came into existence and where it first appeared in human history. In trying to determine the origins of HIV/AIDS, Lyn Frumkin and John Leonard assert,

> An AIDS-like virus causing Simian Acquired Immunodeficiency Syndrome in monkeys has been isolated. A different retrovirus related to HIV has been isolated recently from wild Africa have found cases of unexplained opportunistic infections in patients as early as 1975, that today would meet the current CDC definition of AIDS. It seems likely that the current epidemic may have first occurred somewhere in Central Africa in the mid-1970s.[114]

---

[112] Betty Clare Moffatt, *When Someone You Know Has AIDS: A Book of Hope for Family and Friends* (Santa Monica, CA: IBS, 1986), 34.

[113] Ibid., 35.

[114] Lyn Robert Frumkin and John Martin Leonard, *Questions & Answers on AIDS* (Oradell, NJ: Medical Economics, 1987), 12.

The speculation of the origins is likely to go on for years.

The hypothesis cannot be proven; however, some scientists speculate that AIDS first appeared in America among homosexuals. Frumkin and Leonard write,

> In mid-1981, usual opportunistic infections began to occur in homosexuals and users of intravenous drugs in United States. The infections proved to be uniformly fatal and unprecedented in severity in these previously healthy individuals. This apparently new condition was named the Acquired Immunodeficiency Syndrome, or AIDS.[115]

The claim about its origin cannot be proven. Its origin, mutation, nature, and weaknesses continue to baffle scientists, though hypotheses about origin and nature have shed some glimpses of light.

Some hypotheses point to Dugas, who is believed to have contracted HIV in the jungle of Cameroon through contact with chimps and then brought the disease to North America. David Quammen asserts, "As evidence now shows, HIV had already arrived in North America when Gaëtan Dugas was a virginal adolescent. "Using molecular genetics, researchers have now traced the exact strain of HIV that became a pandemic—HIV-1, Group M, Subtype B—to its original source. Amazingly, through examination of genetic samples from humans and chimps, Quammen reveals scientists have found exactly when and where AIDS started—even a probable theory as to how."[116] Even with recent research and assertions, there is no single evidence of HIV/AIDS' origin. It remains the most mysterious and complex known disease and is incurable. The claim by Quammen that they have found exactly when and where AIDS originated is not accurate and cannot strongly be substantiated.

---

[115] Ibid., 1.

[116] David Quammen, *The Chimp and the River: How AIDS Emerged from the African Forest* (New York: W. W. Norton and Company, 2015), 12.

Transmission of HIV/AIDS

The majority of HIV/AIDS infection occurs through sexual intercourse with infected persons. Promiscuous heterosexuals lead the highest infections of HIV/AIDS. Hans Jager explains,

> In addition, men who often go with prostitutes are great potential carriers of the infection. And as observed over and over again, this investigation shows that with women, the ratio of HIV-positive (40.6%) is higher than men (33.7%). Possibly this finding is attributable to widespread prostitution amongst women and the associated increased risk of infection.[117]

Women are at a higher risk of HIV/AIDS infection than men, especially in Zimbabwe because they are the more vulnerable subculture. In recent decades, prostitution has accelerated HIV/AIDS infections. Diane Richardson writes,

> Most people catch HIV/AIDS through having sex with someone who is already infected with the virus. Vaginal or anal intercourse carries a high risk of infection. Other ways of having sex, such as oral sex, also may be risky if they allow body fluids, such as blood, semen and vaginal secretions, containing the virus to enter the body.[118]

The risk of contracting HIV/AIDS is very high in people that engage in casual sex. Frumkin and Leonard explain,

> Both blood and semen carry the virus in infected persons. To develop AIDS, it is thought that the virus

---

[117] Hans Jager, *AIDS and AIDS Risk Patient Care* (New York: Ellis Horwood, 1988), 80.
[118] Diane Richardson, *Women and AIDS* (New York: Methuen, 1988), 15.

must make its way into the bloodstream and infect lymphocytes. Infected blood or semen can presumably find its way through small breaks in the linings of the mouth, rectum, and perhaps even through skin.[119]

HIV/AIDS transmission also occurs through using needles previously used by an infected person. HIV/AIDS can be transmitted if unsterilized needles are shared.

In some cases, transmission can take place through pregnancy, child-mother transmissions, or through breastfeeding. If a mother is infected with HIV/AIDS, she will likely give birth to an infected baby.

Blood transfusions are another way in which HIV/AIDS may be contracted. If a pregnant woman loses too much blood during delivery, if a person needs blood after being involved in an accident, or even during surgery, when unscreened donated blood is used in transfusion, infections can occur. However, the risk of getting HIV/AIDS infection through blood products has dramatically reduced in recent years.

The reason why HIV infections for women in Africa are rising higher than men is that women are treated as inferiors socially, economically, and legally, due to traditional and cultural trends. Musa Wenkosi Dube asserts,

> Women and young girls are more often than not denied the right to property ownership, decision-making and education in patriarchal societies. They become dependent to their husbands, lovers, brothers, uncles or fathers, and are unable to fend for themselves. They have no control over their bodies and therefore are unable to insist on safer sex. ... Violence in the home, fueled by acceptable gender inequalities, often leaves many women afraid to call for abstinence in relationships.[120]

---

[119] Frumkin and Leonard, *Questions and Answers*, 33.
[120] Musa Wenkosi Dube, *The HIV & AIDS Bible* (Chicago: University of Chicago Press, 2008, 103.

Although one would not agree with all of Dube's perceptions, it is true that the African women for centuries have been denigrated in their respective cultures and traditions. Men tend to dominate women's sexuality (including young girls) in Africa, which puts them at high risk. Many are raped or coerced into sexual relations because of cultural trends or merely for survival. Violence against women is rampant in Africa because of the culture. Dube writes,

> Although many women are becoming infected via their male sex partners . . . women are also threatened with HIV transmission through the smoking of 'crack' cocaine. Sexual favors may be exchanged for the drugs, thus exposing these women to HIV via multiple sex partners.[121]

Women with HIV/AIDS in Zimbabwe face many challenges, especially if they have children. They struggle to take care of themselves and their children who may also be HIV/AIDS positive. They suffer from depression and stress as they become widows; not having income to support their family or to send their children to school. Some women resort to prostitution or cross borders to neighboring countries to buy and sell goods; however, while doing such businesses, they are coerced into sexual relations with HIV/AIDS infected partners. Poverty also forces HIV/AIDS positive women to encourage their daughters to find partners in order to get financial support, thus exposing them to child-sex workers. Ezekiel Kalipeni, Karen Flynn, and Cynthia Pope explain,

> In many cases, women find themselves in economically dependent relationships with men whereby they must stay in risky situations to be able to feed themselves and, very often, their children. Young women are often married too early without regard to their potential or actual educational achievement and are generally prevented from partaking in economically

---

[121] Ibid., 155.

gainful activities that might lend them a semblance of empowerment. Their economic and social vulnerability is often made worse by the lack of formal education investment in them, which leaves them without access to information vital to their overall reproductive health, including but not limited to, knowledge and prevention of diseases such as AIDS.[122]

The challenges that HIV/AIDS positive women and girls face are compounded by the unavailability of antiviral drugs and medications; they do not have easy access to antiviral drugs because of the prejudice associated with the disease. Almond suggests, "In the case of this argument, the issue shifts from the interest of women to the interest of the community, so that the issue becomes: should pregnant women be treated as means to other people's ends?"[123] As far as the moral argument about women is concerned, they should be treated with dignity and respect not as objects to be used as machines to bear children for men. This is morally wrong and categorically inhumane.[124]

Some social taboos may be oppressive to women and are compounded by patriarchal and conservative systems that have been in place for thousands of years. The church faces a dilemma in how to confront and reset Christian teaching of equality, freedom, submission, love, fairness, and mutual respect for women in the church and society.

Medical Consequences of HIV/AIDS

The medical consequences of HIV/AIDS are immense. Decades of research has attempted to find a prevention and cure for HIV/AIDS. Almond asserts,

---

[122] Ezekiel Kalipeni, Karen Flynn, and Cynthia Pope, *Strong Women, Dangerous Times* (New York: Nova Science, 2009), 2.

[123] Brenda Almond, *AIDS—A Moral Issue: The Ethical, Legal and Social Aspects* (New York: St. Martin's, 1990), 44.

[124] Ibid., 45.

HIV consists of two main elements, an outer membrane or envelope, and an inner core. The outer membrane is taken from the cells of the person it infects. As a result, the virus survives extremely poorly outside the body. The infection caused by the virus is a productive infection, in which new virus particles are being produced for all or most of the duration of infection. This means the person is infectious for life.[125]

The HIV/AIDS positive person becomes infectious in weeks after becoming infected and before the immune's response develops into AIDS.

When the virus destroys the infected person's immune system, the person is prone to various other diseases. Shepherd and Smith propound,

The virus is matter which border by definition between living and nonliving material. They are actually replicable protein matter which exists in a parasitic sense and can survive only as long as their hosts exist. HIV belongs to a class known as retroviruses because its reproduction process involves the virus using its reverse transcriptase enzyme to replicate its RNA into DNA molecules.[126]

The HIV virus is complex, and its medical consequences have great impact both in the medical field and to the infected persons.

The available HIV/AIDS drugs (antiviral drugs) do not effectively kill the HIV virus; instead, they slow the progression of the disease in the body. Smith explains,

---

[125] Almond, *AIDS*, 27.
[126] Shepherd Smith and Anita Moreland Smith, "Christians in the Age of AIDS," accessed May 2, 2012, http://www.allbookstores.com/Christians-Age-AIDS-Shepherd-Smith.

The white blood cells that the virus attacks are T4 lymphocytes, monocytes, and macrophages. The invading virus turns the monocytes and macrophages into virus-producing factories for the rest of the individual's life but does not significantly damage the cell. Meanwhile, the T4 lymphocytes are systematically killed off over time.[127]

When the virus destroys the infected person's immune system, the person is prone to various other diseases. AIDS is a complex disease in which the virus unpredictably mutates so that it is difficult to find a medication that could destroy and eliminate its incubation in the body. Almond purports,

> The key biological property of HIV is its specific attack on certain cells of the body, the T 'helper' cells and macrophages of the immune system; this leads to its capacity to cause disease. . . . Thus, individual risk is a function not only of what subpopulation they belong to but which one their partners is from, or has had contact with, and so on.[128]

Almond continues,

> HIV antibody testing has therefore been used as a surrogate for the infection itself, since anyone who develops antibodies must have acquired persistent infection, given the nature of HIV. Following infection people are initially asymptomatic for several years and may remain so indefinitely; some have enlarged lymph nodes. HIV causes progressive damage to immune system or nervous system, leading to symptomatic disease.[129]

---

[127] Ibid.

[128] Almond, *AIDS—A Moral Issue*, 27.

[129] Ibid., 31.

HIV develops into AIDS, which leads to severe damage to cell-mediated immunity that exposes the patient to opportunistic infections. As the patient would be susceptible to minor opportunistic infections and his/her immunity is compromised because of the HIV infection, he/she cannot resist any disease that can attack—so even a disease that is normally not fatal can easily cause death.

Prevention of HIV/AIDS

HIV/AIDS prevention demands teamwork as well as individual responsibility to prevent the spread of the disease. As such, strategies have been discovered that can help to combat HIV/AIDS infections and prevent the spread of the disease. Epidemic infection of HIV/AIDS is caused by various reasons. Land gives suggests,

> These young people, lacking other means of support, may engage in sex in exchange for food, money, drugs, or shelter. In addition, children who have histories of sexual and physical abuse may lack the self-esteem to insist on safer sex even when they are aware of the risks. . . . Many homeless women who test positive for HIV trade sex for money and drugs. Despite widespread fear of HIV transmission by prostitutes, women who have sex with men for drugs or money are likely to infect them.[130]

Regardless of the challenges that are mentioned above, preventive methods must be initiated to curb the spread of the disease.

HIV/AIDS prevention education is critical and necessary to buffer the spread of the disease. HIV/AIDS prevention education must be provided through literature, television, radio, and all social media. Prevention education must also be provided through seminars, conferences in churches, schools, prisons, the community and in companies and

---

[130] Helen Land, *AIDS: A Complete Guide to Psychosocial Intervention* (Milwaukee: Family Service America, 1992), 188.

organizations. Outreach efforts in the streets, communities, and homeless shelters are fundamental in prevention campaigns because public announcements on television and radio cannot be heard or seen by homeless people or those who do not have access to the media. Behavioral changes of sexual habits, such as prostitution, unprotected sex, adultery, fornication, and homosexuality, as well as reducing drug abuse, have been found to decrease HIV/AIDS infections.

For those already infected, an ideal drug to combat AIDS must be used. Scientists have discovered anti-viral drugs that boost the immune system. The HIV Treatment Information Base reposts,

> CD4 cells are a type of lymphocytes (white blood cell). They are an important part of the immune system. CD4 cells are sometimes called T-Cells. The normal ranges for CD4 and CD8 counts varies depending on the lab and test, but for an HIV negative person a normal CD4 count is in the range 460 to 1600.[131]

Jager points out,

> Retrovirus, of which HIV is one, is situated as to build their genetic information into the gene bank of cell. When there is a failure to kill the virus or eliminate it from the body, replication of the virus should be arrested by a drug (virus stasis) or it should be prevented from attacking cells.[132]

This is important information for patients to take heed and apply. When medication has failed to cure AIDS, prevention must be emphasized in order to prevent the severe complications of opportunistic infections.

Adequate information on infections is critical for HIV/AIDS prevention.

---

[131] HIV Treatment Information Base, September 19, 2014, accessed October 5, 2016, www.*i-base.info.*

[132] Jager, *AIDS*, 40.

The use of sterile disposable needles prevents infection and use of condoms has been found effective if used. As a model to combat the spread of HIV/AIDS, pre and post-counseling is one of the means to help those with the disease. In pre-counseling, the counselor sits down with the counselee who is seeking to know his/her HIV/AIDS status before testing. In post-counseling, the counselee has completed the testing and is ready to receive the results. Post-counseling has some challenges, especially if the counselee is HIV/AIDS positive. If he/she is HIV/AIDS positive, the person is advised what to eat and how to live a healthy life, where, when, and how the antiviral drugs can be taken, and how they can help to boost immunity. If the test results are negative, the individual is given information and advised to prevent him/herself from contracting the disease.

Inoculation is another form of HIV/AIDS prevention. Jager asserts,

> Even in viral epidemics, this measure has proved an ideal weapon against a virus disease. Smallpox and infantile paralysis were eradicated by this means. . . . HIV displays some peculiarities which render the development of a vaccine extraordinarily difficult. The external protein coating of HIV defeats established transformations by spontaneous mutation. This can be a historically important development in the virus's mechanism, so as to elude the antibodies directed against it by the immune system by changing the surface structures.[133]

Prevention is better than the cure. Prevention of the spread of HIV/AIDS is vital and needs to be spearheaded by church leaders.

Additionally, breastfeeding can be avoided to prevent mother-to-child transmission of HIV/AIDS. Antiviral drugs have also been developed to prevent the transmission of HIV/AIDS while the child in still in the womb. The drug helps to prevent numerous infections of babies with HIV/AIDS. The next section discusses the treatment of HIV/AIDS.

---

[133] Jager, *AIDS*, 38.

Treatment of HIV/AIDS

Currently no treatment is available to destroy HIV/AIDS or restore the immune system. Richardson contends, "Research on antiviral drugs is being carried out in the United States and other countries in an attempt to provide a cure. Antiviral drugs are substances which interfere with the growth of reproduction viruses."[134] The challenge with antiviral drugs is that they often do not discriminate between infected cells and healthy cells Richardson continues,

> Another problem is that HIV is capable of infecting cells in the brain and other parts of the central nervous system. If an antiviral drug is not capable of passing through into the cerebrospinal fluid or the brain, and most are not, these infected cells may continue to produce more viruses.[135]

Antiviral drugs will continue to be a challenge because they cannot get rid of the HIV virus or they cannot utterly destroy all the infected cells.

The other drug that has been tested to put the infection into remission is Ribavarin. This drug can slow down the multiplication of HIV in the body. Richardson writes, "Further research is under way to assess its possible usefulness in the treatment of AIDS. Tests on the other antiviral agents, such as Suramin, HPA-23, and Ansamycin, have also demonstrated a reduction in the amount of virus present."[136] Antivirus drugs can significantly help to reduce or slow down the multiplication of the virus in the body of the infected person, but none of the drugs tested can cure AIDS.

HIV/AIDS educational programs can be part of the prevention of the disease. Siegel points out,

---

[134] Richardson, *Women and AIDS*, 23.
[135] Ibid.
[136] Ibid.

Educational programs for staff, patients and families can provide accurate information to deal with real and imagined anxieties. . . . More importantly, safer sex practice and no needle sharing should be practiced by everyone to prevent a whole variety of diseases, of which AIDS is the most serious.[137]

HIV/AIDS educational programs must be used to buffer further infections of the disease.

The use of the antiviral drugs, which can influence the immune system, are continually tested. Richardson continues,

Some of these immune-boosting drugs, such as Interfero. Others, like Cyclosporin, acts by suppressing the immune system. This latter approach to treatment stems from the theory that HIV works by tricking the immune system by destroying itself. . . . Made by Burroughs Wellcome, AZT has been tested mainly on AIDS patients who have pneumocystis. ATZ is not a cure for AIDS. Although it stops the virus from multiplying, it does not destroy it.[138]

Although there is no cure for AIDS, opportunistic infections can be treated. Moffatt asserts,

There can be some improvements in AIDS conditions when the sound principles of nutrition, exercise, and following medical recommendations of the attending physician. Some AIDS persons have used the following to help fortify their immune systems and to create a more favorable climate for detoxification of existing viruses. Immuneplex, large doses of Vitamin C, Spirulina and LaPacho tea.[139]

[137] Larry Siegel, *AIDS and Substance Abuse* (New York: Haworth, 1987), 15.
[138] Richardson, *Women and AIDS*, 24.
[139] Moffatt, *When Someone You Love Has AIDS*, 131.

Healthy eating and exercise do not cure but can help to boost the patient's immune system. Good diet helps HIV/AIDS patients live healthy lives even though they are infected. Moffatt writes, "Until a cure is found for AIDS and all its opportunistic manifestations, anything and everything that can increase the well-being of the AIDS person and help each one to rebuild his body defenses can be utilized with opportunistic results."[140] The following sections discuss the mythical beliefs about HIV/AIDS.

MYTHICAL

Myths about Origin

Myths about the origin of HIV/AIDS vary from place to place and culture to culture with many similarities across Africa. These myths are not well documented since they are part of an oral tradition that circulates without validation or authentication. As such, this section discussed even unpublished materials as sources of oral tradition and myths about HIV/AIDS.

According to mythical beliefs, the origin of HIV/AIDS has to do with the angry gods and spirits who are orchestrating curses upon bad human beings. The myths say gods and spirits eliminate bad people among the good people through cursing them with AIDS. The gods and the spirits use witchcraft and evil spirits to punish bad people in the community. Richmond and Gestrin write,

> Related to witchcraft in Africa is a widely held belief that things do not happen unless someone wishes them to happen. The reaction to misfortune is to ask why and blame personal misfortunes on the actions of the wicked people, evil spirits, and the witches in order to seek the

---

[140] Ibid., 132.

cause of the unfortunate and why it is happening and then remove it.[141]

Accordingly, they believe everything that happens to an individual or community, whether it is good or bad, is connected to the spirits. HIV/AIDS is viewed as a curse to an individual, family, or community. Richmond and Gestrin continue, "When, in 1995, the Ebola virus spread to Kikwit, a Congo city of 400,000, some local inhabitants though that evil spirits had struck."[142] Belief in the power of the spirits in Africa is a reality across the continent, except if someone is a true Christian.

Another mythical belief about the origins of HIV/AIDS, in Africa in general is that the HIV/AIDS virus was chemically devised and designed by Westerners as a biological weapon to eradicate black people in order that they would control world population. There is no tangible proof and evidence to substantiate the claim of the argument, but the myth is well known.

Simple ignorance and misconceptions have arisen to justify or mystify the origin of HIV/AIDS. There is still the mythical belief that homosexual people are responsible for bringing HIV/AIDS to Africa; homosexuality is believed to be animalistic and is unacceptable behavior and an unacceptable lifestyle in African culture and tradition. The myth describes homosexuals as abnormal people who have resorted to animal behavior and are doomed to join evil spirits in hell when they die.

Still another myth that circulates in the African culture regarding the origin of AIDS is that man had sex with animals that resulted in the incurable disease and came as a punishment to all humanity from God of heaven (Mvelinqangi). Mvelinqangi is angry with all men; hence the scourge.

Mosquito bites have also been mythically responsible for infecting and transmitting HIV/AIDS to people. As transmitters of AIDS, according to the myth, mosquitoes are believed to bite other species

---

[141] Yale Richmond and Phyllis Gestrin, *Into Africa: Intercultural Insights* (Yarmouth, ME: Intercultural, 1998), 38.
[142] Ibid., 39.

of animals and also suck the bark of unknown trees and carry diseases to human beings. None of these myths about the origin of HIV/AIDS have any scientific support.

Myths about Transmission

There are also numerous unfounded myths about how HIV/AIDS is transmitted. Richardson dismisses several of the myths about transmission of the disease:

> You cannot catch HIV simply by being near, eating with, or touching a person who is infected by it. Nor will you catch HIV by touching objects used by someone who has the virus. No one has ever become infected through swimming in the same pool used by infected persons, through sharing clothes or towels, or through drinking out of the same cup as them. . . . There is absolutely no reason to think that it can be spread through the air or by casual social contacts.[143]

No evidence indicates that it is unsafe to play, work, or socialize with those infected.

Additionally, there is also no evidence that HIV transmission may infect someone through a person's urine, feces, tears, or sweat. One cannot get HIV through coughing, spitting, or sneezing. HIV/AIDS cannot survive on surfaces such as toilet seats, door handles, cutlery, or tables.

Myths about Consequences

Myths about HIV/AIDS consequences confuse the truth about HIV/AIDS and the ability to help curb the spread of the disease. Some believe in the myths and contract HIV/AIDS as they dismiss the reality of the

---

[143] Richardson, *Women and AIDS*, 14.

disease. They do not protect themselves from the disease because they falsely assume that the improved antiretroviral drugs are a cure for the disease. The misconception and misunderstanding of the true benefits of the drugs derail prevention.

In contrast to what some think about HIV/AIDS's effects, the antiretroviral drugs do not cure HIV/AIDS. The myth that the antiretroviral drugs can cure HIV/AIDS positive people is a fallacy.

These myths lead to panic. Jager explains, "Anxiety may also be manifested as phobia, compulsive thoughts of dying and death, fear of loss of sexual appetite, etc. These reactions and their duration vary to an extreme degree and can lead to breakdown in day-to-day living."[144] For many, anxiety turns into panic. HIV/AIDS has been misunderstood, misinterpreted, and exaggerated to a greater extent than diseases such as cancer and other infectious diseases.

Myths about Prevention

Despite anxiety over consequences, myths about prevention of HIV/AIDS hamper efforts to stop its spread. Land provides an example:

> Some men believe that the partner who is penetrated anally is gay, whereas the other partner is straight. Because these men do not perceive themselves as gay, they may feel that they are not at risk of contracting HIV and thus ignore the literature, posters, classes, or other educational material aimed at gay and bisexual men.[145]

Myths about prevention have plunged individuals, families, and communities into misconceptions and beliefs that increase the HIV/AIDS infections:

---

[144] Jager, *AIDS*, 129.
[145] Land, *AIDS*, 189.

Negative values and relationships examining the contexts of behavior, including policy environment, and society, the position of women in society relative to decisions about sexuality, and the spirituality, and the spiritual contexts the health behavior in question.[146]

Myths about HIV/AIDS prevention has stiffened the efforts to curb the spread of the disease and has opened more promiscuity with people thinking it is preventable, but that it is not true.

Myths about Treatment

Myths about HIV/AIDS treatment has gone beyond ethical and moral reasoning. A change of sexual habits is one of the measures to prevent the spread of HIV/AIDS infections. Myths about HIV/AIDS infection treatment has circulated large and wide and it buffers progress on research. AIDS fear and phobia escalate the myths about treatment. Jager asserts, "Particularly marked amongst the heterosexual population is the so-called 'AIDS phobia', an unequivocal and severe neurotic disorder, which can and must be treated by psychotherapy. The fear of the disease is thus essentially a desire."[147] The phobia that Jager alludes to has caused a number of abuses to various groups of people. Psychological stress is a breeding ground for fear of the unknown. The driving force is the fear of AIDS stigmatization.

Jager continues to write about the driving force of phobia and fear about HIV/AIDS treatment:

Most of those who have a positive test result react first of all with hopelessness, fear and loss of self-control. While they perceive their bodies as unreliable and

---

[146] O. Airhihenbuwa Collins and DeWitt J. Webster, "Culture and African Contexts of HIV/AIDS Prevention, Care and Support," *Sahara-J: Journal of Social Aspects of HIV/AIDS* 1, no. 1 (2004): 8, accessed June 23, 2016, http://dx.doi.org/10.1080/17290376.2004.9724822.

[147] Jager, *AIDS*, 129.

dangerous, as the plaything of a hostile fate, fear mounts through thoughts being limited to the negative side, an increasing burden to live the already weakened immune defenses.[148]

Fear of dying overwhelms patients and then they resort to mythical treatments that are not credible and are unfounded. The principles of love, forgiveness, acceptance, and oneness with God gives health and inner peace.

In some parts of Africa, people think that having sex with an albino will cure HIV/AIDS. As a result, many HIV/AIDS infected people who believe this myth, go around having sex with albinos. Some of the myths suggest that if an HIV/AIDS positive male has sex with a virgin girl, he will be cured of the disease. Consequently, many young and innocent girls are raped and have been victims of predators who seek a cure. Some HIV/AIDS positive people have also been prosecuted for raping infants as young as four months old in hope of cure of HIV/AIDS. The moral and ethical decisions made by some HIV/AIDS positive people have gone beyond norms and have created a cultural menace in Africa.

Another myth suggests that people who are HIV/AIDS infected can safely have children. The truth of the matter is that it is possible for an HIV/AIDS positive pregnant woman to have a child free of HIV/AIDS, provided the pregnant women takes antiretroviral therapy (ART) during her pregnancy; however, there is no guarantee of no transmission. Although medications are effective in preventing the replication of HIV in the body, there is no cure for AIDS, but prevention is better than a cure.

CULTURAL

The following section discusses the cultural stigma, impact, cultural corrective and biblical corrective in regard to families, women, children, and discipleship as to how each has been negatively affected by the

---

[148] Jager, *AIDS*, 130.

myths. In the same vein, the section discusses the cultural corrective that gives accurate information to improve both physical and spiritual health. The section concludes with the discussion about biblical corrective on which biblical standards could decrease transmission of the disease and improve discipleship in the church and the hope in Christ.

Cultural Stigma

The cultural stigma of HIV/AIDS poses challenges to individuals, families, and communities since HIV/AIDS affects both the individual who contracts it as well as the families and communities to which the individual belongs. Hoffman writes,

> Questions of confidentiality and the maintenance of personal privacy, living with uncertainty in the face of life-threating illness, difficulties in acquiring life assurance, stigma and isolation were all subject familiar to those with hemophilia and how their families before the onset of AIDS.[149]

Families of HIV/AIDS positive people at the center of pain and suffering with their loved ones face the indignation of cultural stigma.

The HIV/AIDS pandemic has caused pervasive and chronic grief to people with HIV/AIDS. Land explains,

> Figures can't convey the pain and loss experienced by those affected personally by this epidemic. Those who are affected by AIDS grieve continuously. In addition, the stigma attached to HIV/AIDS and the young ages of persons who contract the disease create special

---

[149] Mary Ann Hoffman, *Counseling Clients with HIV Disease* (New York: Guilford, 1996), 34.

bereavement issues for both persons living with the disease and practitioners.[150]

Grief and pain affects all family members and the community at large because African families in Zimbabwe are interconnected culturally. Grief affects the whole community as the neighbors grieve and comfort one another during infection and after the death of a person living with HIV/AIDS. Land states, "Grief is a normal and natural adaptive response to loss. It affects our thoughts, feelings, behaviors, physical and well-being, and spirit. It is both an interpersonal and intrapersonal process."[151] The HIV/AIDS stigma that includes homophobia, social condemnation, lack of social support, and cultural isolation drive the wave of the cultural impact of HIV/AIDS pandemic.

The cultural stigma of HIV/AIDS victims causes segregation and prejudice that leaves victims culturally isolated and barred from social interactions with others. Land continues, "Individuals and communities living with HIV/AIDS face an inordinate amount of psychological distress. Stressors include a sustained threat to life and physical integrity, threat and harm to loved ones, destruction of the community, and numerous deaths."[152] When one suffers, the whole community suffers. Cultural stigma ripples like waves in African communities because they believe they are one and share pain and joy together as a people, even in times of HIV/AIDS infections.

Cultural Impact

Beyond the stigma, HIV/AIDS negatively influences the culture. Hoffman contends,

> HIV disease is not simply a physical entity. Rather, the impact of the disease is reflected in many other

---

[150] Land, *AIDS*, 239.
[151] Land, *AIDS*, 239.
[152] Ibid., 241.

important ways, such as in emotional responses, copying strategies, self-image, and changes in life goals. But the physical aspects of the disease often lead to the first awareness that something is amiss; then they become markers of the relentless progression of the disease.[153]

Almond concurs with Hoffman that HIV is not simply a physical issue: "AIDS raises a number of ethical and social problems which must inevitably be confronted by the whole community, by people with AIDS and their relatives, and by those professionally involved."[154] It is a physical, moral, and emotional disease because when one is infected with HIV/AIDS, the family, relatives, church, and community all are affected. When the virus destroys the infected person's immune system, the person is prone to various diseases.

Women are the pillars of African homes and are known for their wisdom in advising their husbands and children, but when crisis strikes at home, they are left confused, stranded, helpless, and hopeless with the future, especially if their husbands were the bread winners of their families. HIV/AIDS has decimated family ties, values, resources, relationships, and hopes for the future. When the husband dies of HIV/AIDS and if the wife is also HIV/AIDS positive, her predicament is compounded and presents a dire future with the lack of basic needs to fend her children, which can lead to depression.

Women in Africa have a higher rate of HIV infections than men because women are treated as inferior socially, economically, and legally due to traditional and cultural trends. Men tend to dominate women's sexuality in Africa, which puts them at high risk. Many women and young girls are raped or coerced into sexual relations. Violence against women is rampant in Africa because of culture.

Women with HIV/AIDS face many challenges, especially if they have children. They struggle to take care of themselves and their children, who may also be HIV/AIDS positive. They suffer from

---

[153] Hoffman, *Counseling Clients*, 1.
[154] Almond, *Aids—A Moral Issue*, 33.

depression and stress as they become widows and may have no income to feed their family or send their children to school. Some women resort to prostitution or cross borders to neighboring countries to buy and sell goods, but while doing such businesses are coerced into sexual relations with HIV/AIDS infected partners. Poverty also forces HIV/AIDS positive women to encourage their daughters to find partners in order to get financial support, thus exposing them to child-sex workers. Kalipeni, Flynn and Pope write,

> In many cases, women find themselves in economically dependent relationships with men whereby they must stay in risky situations to be able to feed themselves and, very often, their children. Young women are often married too early without regard to their potential or actual educational achievement and are generally prevented from partaking in economically gainful activities that might lend them a semblance of empowerment. Their economic and social vulnerability is often made worse by the lack of formal education investment in them, which leaves them without access to information vital to their overall reproductive health, including but not limited to, knowledge and prevention of diseases such as AIDS.[155]

The challenges that HIV/AIDS positive women and girls face are compounded by the unavailability of antiviral drugs and other medications.

Social taboos are suppressive to women and compounded by thousands of years of patriarchal and conservative systems. The church has a dilemma as to how to confront and reset Christian teaching of equality, freedom, submission, love, fairness, and mutual respect for women in the church and society. HIV/AIDS is about life and death. Women have been drawn into the arena of the sex industry by

---

[155] Kalipeni, Flynn, and Pope, *Strong Women, Dangerous Times*, 2.

poverty, marginalization, and inequality in society and most third world countries. Kalipeni, Flynn and Pope explain,

> The sex industry, previously considered marginal, has come to occupy a strategic and central position in the developing of international capitalism in which millions of women and children have been converted into sexual commodities through commercial sex work, wars, expansion of the tourist industry, the growth and normalization of pornography, and internationalization of arranged marriages.[156]

Women face these challenges and HIV/AIDS has impacted and exacerbated the stigma and suffering of women.

Children face the greatest challenge as they are vulnerable to abuse because of the HIV/ADS pandemic. HIV/AIDS has caused havoc, frustration, disunity, disintegration of families and it has brought misery, hopelessness, helplessness, and confusion on the definition of a family. In Africa, an ideal family has a mother and a father. However, it is still defined as a family if the father, who is the head of the household, dies and leaves his wife and the children behind. Many homes are child-headed because of parents who have died because of HIV/AIDS. In such a scenario, children are left exposed to child abuse, such as rape, confiscation of inherited property, hunger, commercial sex, prostitution, child-labor, poverty, drop out of school, and other misfortunes.

Church/discipleship is negatively affected by the prevalent myths that circulate. Dismissing the myths promulgated across the culture is a challenge that makes church/discipleship difficult in evangelizing and discipling converts. Almond writes,

> Naturally AIDS has given rise to great anxiety and considerable fear everywhere, largely because there was, and still is in some quarters, a lot of ignorance about AIDS. There is always fear of the unknown, and more

---

[156] Ibid., 19.

so when the illness has such terrible effects and is at the moment incurable.[157]

Inaccurate information about HIV/AIDS accentuates fear and anxiety in the society. Almond continues,

> The Church will only be able to respond in the proper way to AIDS if we resist the tide of fear and hysteria which is accompanying the spread of AIDS but it has always been the job of the Church to take a stand against superstition and mythology. Initially, any theological reflections will be concerned with the sufferers, and those sufferers are our fellow human beings, men, women and children.[158]

The spread of genuine and reliable information is needed to foster truth and to improve discipleship within the church. This is to enhance the truth about AIDS and the accurate information about its existence, infections, and transmission.

Cultural Corrective

A cultural corrective on the HIV/AIDS stigma will bring a new perception about those living with HIV/AIDS thus giving opportunities for a Christian response to treat those living with HIV/AIDS in a God-honoring way. This should result in those living with HIV/AIDS feeling loved and cared for and retaining their dignity as image-bearers of God.

The cultural corrective needs to include accurate information on the origin and transmission of HIV/AIDS. In particular, there needs to be a concerted effort to correct inaccurate teaching of African Traditional religion healers who profit from using charms and herbs without any

---

[157] Almond, *AIDS-A Moral Issue*, 153.
[158] Ibid., 154.

effect on the disease. The lack of accurate information and adequate health care contribute to the problem. Almond explains,

> Given these realities, it begins to be more understandable that people would believe the myths about HIV, such as the belief that sex with a virgin can cure AIDS. In the absence of formal health care, many poor people turn to traditional healers, who may be a cross between a doctor and a minister.[159]

Properly informed Christian leaders could engage with community leaders to pass on accurate information and dispel the myths of the traditional healers.

This changed perception could also engage the society's traditional beliefs regarding women and children, which should result in them being less vulnerable to HIV/AIDS. Almond writes,

> In most developing countries of the world, women have few rights and choices in life. Many countries give them little legal protection, and most societies view them as being responsible for making their husband happy, bearing children and caring for the families.[160]

Bourke describes the result:

> Certain customs in Africa have contributed to the spread of HIV/AIDS, especially through families. When a woman's husband dies, she and her children are "inherited" along with his property. According to some traditions, she is expected to become the wife of

---

[159] Almond, *AIDS-A Moral Issue*, 83.
[160] Ibid., 81.

one of her late husband's relatives, or to be purified of her husband's death through sex.[161]

If either partner in this new marriage is HIV positive, the disease can continue to spread.

Biblical Corrective

While cultural changes can have some impact, a biblical corrective is desperately needed, which could change the church's response to persons with HIV/AIDS so that they might experience hope in Christ. By recognizing the value and dignity of each image-bearer of God, even those who are HIV positive can experience God's love through the church. By changing the church's perspective, the redemptive plan of God can be shared with those who have been stigmatized with HIV/AIDS as the church carries out the Great Commission given by Christ.

Not only will cultural changes make a difference in the lives of those with HIV/AIDS, a biblical corrective will help the church to take responsibility to live out Christ's commands to love and care for those in need. There is a Christian duty to serve rather than shun those in need. By demonstrating love and leading others to properly to respond to HIV/AIDS positive people, the church can bring glory to God while serving God's image-bearers. Nicolson points out the fundamental message for the church:

> As well as being prophetic church recalling humans to live under the law of God, the church is to be an evangelizing church bringing the news of God's love. . . . Evangelism means more than talking about the good news of God's love. It means making the good news come true.[162]

---

[161] Dale Hanson Bourke, *Responding to HIV/AIDS* (Downers Grove, IL: IVP, 2013), 79.

[162] Bourke, *Responding to HIV/AIDS*, 178.

A biblical corrective will not only affect the HIV/AIDS population and the church, it could affect society at-large by reinforcing the God-given institution of marriage, which has been perverted by man. DeYoung explains the standard:

> It is about Jesus's view of marriage, and the point of Roman 1, and the sin of Genesis 19. . . . It is about faith and repentance, and heaven and hell and a hundred other things. . . . In the traditional view, marriage is the union between a man and a woman. That is what marriage is, before the state confers any benefit on it. Marriage, in the traditional view, is a *prepolitical institution*.[163]

Since sex is a primary way of transmission of HIV/AIDS, the biblical corrective needs to address intimacy. Burk describes the proper understanding of sex within marriage:

> God's purpose of sex is revealed in the account of God's initial of human beings as male and female (Gen 1-2). That account and subsequence of scriptural reflection on it suggest a very clear purpose for human sexuality. . . . Sex, gender, marriage, manhood and womanhood-all of it-ultimately exist all for the glory of God.[164]

Burk maintains the biblical view that sex is God ordained and must be consummated within marriage. In that way, marriage should be honored by all. Marriage is holy matrimony displaying the relationship between Christ and His church.

---

[163] Kevin Deyoung, *What Does the Bible Say about Homosexuality* (Wheaton, IL: Crossway, 2015), 9.

[164] Denny Burk, *The Meaning of Sex* (Wheaton, IL: Crossway, 2013), 23

CONCLUSION

HIV/AIDS is pandemic in Africa. Rather than medically sound information, myths regarding its origin, transmission, consequences, prevention, and treatment misinform the population. The negative impact of the disease has caused a stigma to be attached to those who test positive, and this negative impact has infected the church. By correcting cultural misconceptions and applying a biblical corrective, the church could bring honor to God and his image-bearers. The teaching plan in chapter 4 promotes accurate information and a God-honoring way for the church to minister to those with HIV/AIDS and the societies from which they come.

— 4 —

TEACHING SERIES/SEMINARS

The teaching plan is designed to train Christian leaders of International Christian Baptist Church and any organization to respond to HIV/AIDS positive people. The target group is the Christian leaders of International Christian Baptist Church and other organizations with similar challenges. The Christian leaders will in turn teach and implement the teaching lessons to change lives of church members to be able to respond to HIV/AIDS positive people in a God-honoring way to relate to God's image-bearers. This chapter presents an overview of the lessons, which are presented in detail in the appendices. The overall plan is to change cognitive, affection, and behavior of Christians so that they may respond to HIV/AIDS positive people in a God-honoring way. *Creative Bible Teaching*, by Lawrence O. Richards and Gary J. Bredfeldt, is used as a model for the lesson plans. They write, "The Bible teacher must build a bridge from the ancient world of the Bible to the modern world of the student. It is a bridge that crosses both time and cultural boundaries. This bridge must take the student into a society far different from his own and back again."[165]

The first offering of the seminar follows the general pattern laid out in chapter 2. At the completion of the teaching series, the course will be modified so that it can be used by various churches and Christian organizations to respond to the HIV/AIDS pandemic. The seminars are

---

[165] Lawrence O. Richard and Gary J. Bredfeldt, *Creative Bible Teaching*, (Chicago: Moody, 1998), 14.

flexible and open to suit the students per African tradition and culture. The seminars will be conducted in a manner to accommodate the volunteers who will give their time and resources to make the seminars successful.

TARGET AUDIENCE

The Christian leaders of International Christ Baptist Church range in age from 25 to 76 years. They have different levels of education— some have master's or bachelor's degrees while others are high school graduates. They also have a variety of job experience—most are teachers, but some are engineers, physicians, nurses, pastors, or civil servants. The Christians leaders who will attend the seminars are all born-again, committed Christians and are ready to serve. With this course of study, they will be able to better understand the truth about the stigmatized HIV/AIDS victims and be better equipped to relate to them in a God-honoring way.

Teaching Plan Overview

Christian leaders are to obey and lead by example to love people living with HIV/AIDS. As covered in the first lesson, the love demonstrated by Christ on the cross in meeting people's ultimate need should be reflected by all Christian believers as they love and care for those in need. Christian leaders will learn the importance of treating all of God's image-bearers with respect, love, and care. Christian leaders will be prepared to lead churches in areas of leadership, compassion, and caring for HIV/AIDS positive people. To help transform the Christian leaders so that, in turn, they might help transform others, a twelve-week teaching series is planned. The overview of those weeks is presented in this chapter and the details of those lessons are presented in the relevant appendices.

Week 1: Loving One Another Is a Demonstration of God's Love

The first week is a lesson on the love of Christ that all Christians are obligated to demonstrate.[166] This love and care extends to outcasts of society and those left out because of their HIV/AIDS status. The text teaches that Christians should love and demonstrate the love Christ by loving one other. The key passage is 1 John 4:7-21, NKJV :

> Beloved, let us love one another, for love is of God; and everyone who loves is born of God and knows God. He who does not loveth does not know God, for God is love. In this the love of God was manifested toward us, that God has sent His only begotten Son into the world, that we might live through Him. In this is love, not that we loved God, but that He loved us and sent His Son *to be* the propitiation for our sins. Beloved, if God so loved us, we also ought to love one another."

Exegetical idea: Christians are commanded to love one another as Christ loved; for love comes from the Father. Whoever loves is born of God and knows God.

Pedagogical idea: The Christian leaders will be taught about the love of God shown and demonstrated through His Son, Jesus Christ, who died on the cross for sins. Therefore, Christians must also demonstrate love and compassion to others.

Week 2: God's Image-Bearers

The teaching on Christian love toward people in I John 4:7-12, NKJV shows God's love in redeeming humanity after the fall.[167] The love of God continues to reach out to those who are still in sin and have not converted to Christianity. God's image-bearers must be treated

---

[166] See appendix 1.
[167] See appendix 2.

with respect and dignity and loved by Christians because God also loves them. The seminar will discuss the reason for the fall and the need for Christian leaders to understand the misery it brought to all humankind. God's image-bearers are redeemed through the death and the resurrection of the second Adam who defeated death. The restoration of God's Image-bearers gives hope to those who believe in Christ. The lesson plan will enhance Christian leaders to develop positive attitudes toward HIV/AIDS positive people.

The lesson will teach about sin and its consequences, the condition of people before God, and redemption through Jesus Christ. The lesson is designed to equip Christian leaders to teach and witness to all kinds of people, regardless of their situations, conditions, ethnicity, race, or background. Christian leaders will learn skills to respond to those living with HIV/AIDS in a God-honoring way that upholds human dignity and respect. The Christian leaders will be able to model Christ's love to those suffering from HIV/AIDS. The key passage is Genesis 1:26-28, NKJV:

> Then God said, "Let Us make man in Our image, according to Our likeness; let them have dominion over the fish of the sea, over the birds of the air, and over the cattle, over all the earth and over every creeping thing that creeps on the earth." So, God created man in His *own* image; in the image of God He created him; male and female He created them. Then God blessed them, and God said to them, "Be fruitful and multiply; fill the earth and subdue it; have dominion over the fish of the sea, over the birds of the air, and over every living thing that moves on the earth."

Exegetical idea: The fall of Adam brought misery to all mankind and there was alienation between God and man because of sin. However, through the death and resurrection of Jesus Christ, hope, reconciliation, and love has been poured out to God's image-bearers.

Pedagogical idea: Christian leaders will be taught that God's image-bearers who are HIV/AIDS positive must be treated with respect and dignity as image-bearers whom Christ died for.

Week 3: God's Redemptive Plan for Humanity

The teaching plan on John 3:16 shows God's love to humanity: after the fall, God sent His one and only Son, Jesus Christ, to save those who believed in Him,[168] which is God's demonstration of His love to His fallen creatures. Appendix 3 details the lesson plan in which the discussion about God's love is unveiled. The Christian leaders will be able to analyze the text and conclude how they would demonstrate the love of Jesus to HIV/AIDS positive people. The love of God is always active and demands Christians to be part of the community to show Christ's love. The Christian leaders attending these seminars will demonstrate their love for Christ and people living with HIV/AIDS. The key passage was John 3:16: "For God so loved the world that He gave His only begotten Son, that whoever believes in Him should not perish but have everlasting life."

Exegetical idea: God's love was demonstrated in the death and the resurrection of Jesus Christ to give eternal life to all those who believe in Him.

Pedagogical idea: The love of God is the epicenter of God's love to reach out to His own people and to reconcile them to Himself as the truth to be taught to all people of the world.

Week 4: Great Commission and Disciple Making

The Great Commission is the call for Christians to make disciples of all nations and to baptize them in union with the Trinity.[169] In week 4, the Christian leaders learned about the importance of evangelism and discipleship. The Great Commission compels Christians to desire to fulfill the commission of Christ Jesus through witnessing everywhere

---

[168] See appendix 3.
[169] See appendix 4.

in the world. The Great Commission was given by Christ to evangelize; the gospel is open to everyone. The Christian leaders will be able to understand their mandate to share the gospel to the lost and to those who are HIV/AIDS positive. Everyone need the gospel because all have sinned and come short of the glory of God. The text explains the love that God has and has shown to all humankind as an outreach to the lost. After the fall in the Garden of Eden, God sought the man and has been seeking him to restore and reconcile with him. The key passage is Matthew 28:18-20, NKJV:

> And Jesus came and spoke to them, saying, "All authority has been given to Me in heaven and on earth. Go therefore and make disciples of all the nations, baptizing them in the name of the Father and of the Son and of the Holy Spirit, teaching them to observe all things that I have commanded you; and lo, I am with you always, *even* to the end of the age." Amen.

Exegetical idea: After Christ's resurrection, He commanded His disciples to make disciples of all nations. Therefore, all Christians are commissioned to make disciples of all nations, teaching and baptizing them in the name of the Father, the Son and the Holy Spirit.

Pedagogical idea: The Great Commission compels Christians to connect with all kinds of people who need Christ's love, forgiveness, and reconciliation and compassion.

Week 5: Restoration and Christian Service

Christ commissioned His disciples to reach out to the lost in order to bring them back to God, and restoring sinners demonstrates how loving God is to have died for sinners.[170] The lesson on restoration ushers a new paradigm of thinking in the church to support and care for outcasts of the community, such as those living with HIV/AIDS. The lesson

---

[170] See appendix 5.

teaches the Christian leaders to be proactive in restoring those who are considered outcasts of the society by embracing them and assimilating them into the church system. Christ met with the Samaritan woman who was despised in the society and shunned, but Christ broke the social barrier and gave her hope. The Christian leaders will learn how to confront social injustices and restore HIV/AIDS positive people back into society with dignity and respect. The lesson will teach how to restore those who are shunned in society because of their conditions or diseases. The key passage is John 4:9-19, NKJV:

> A woman of Samaria came to draw water. Jesus said to her, "Give Me a drink." For His disciples had gone away into the city to buy food. Then the woman of Samaria said to Him, "How is it that You, being a Jew, ask a drink from me, a Samaritan woman?" For Jews have no dealings with Samaritans. Jesus answered and said to her, "If you knew the gift of God, and who it is who says to you, 'Give Me a drink,' you would have asked Him, and He would have given you living water." The woman said to Him, "Sir, you have nothing to draw with, and the well is deep. Where then do You get that living water? Are You greater than our father Jacob, who gave us the well, and drank from it himself, as well as his sons and his livestock?" Jesus answered and said to her, "Whoever drinks of this water will thirst again, but whoever drinks of the water that I shall give him will never thirst. But the water that I shall give him will become in him a fountain of water springing up into everlasting life."

Exegetical idea: Jesus' encounter with the Samaritan woman broke the cross-cultural and social barrier that existed between the Israelites and the Samaritans for centuries in order to show how they should live together in harmony.

Pedagogical idea: Jesus overcame barriers that were based on

Jewish customs, and his model can be applied to the situation in a society through the discrimination against HIV/AIDS positive people.

Week 6: Restoration of the Outcasts

Jesus demonstrates compassion by restoring ten lepers to good health again after He had an encounter with them.[171] In a society where lepers were regarded as unclean and left outside the camp to heal or to die alone, Jesus healed and restored them. The lesson will teach why Christians should be compassionate and embracive to all who are regarded as outcasts and unclean. The Christian leaders will be taught to be open-minded and to welcome those who are rejected by society. The ten lepers are the symbol of hope in Christ. The Christian leaders will be able to help those who are dejected by society because of their sicknesses, such as those living with HIV/AIDS. People living with HIV/AIDS can receive the same hope that the ten lepers received. Christian leaders will be trained to teach hope in Christ. The key passage is Luke 17:12-19, NKJV:

> Then as He entered a certain village, there met Him ten men who were lepers, who stood afar off. And they lifted up their voices and said, "Jesus, Master, have mercy on us!" So, when He saw them, He said to them, "Go, show yourselves to the priests." And so, it was that as they went, they were cleansed. And one of them, when he saw that he was healed, returned, and with a loud voice glorified God, and fell down on his face at His feet, giving Him thanks. And he was a Samaritan. So, Jesus answered and said, "Were there not ten cleansed? But where are the nine? Were there not any found who returned to give glory to God except this foreigner?" 19And He said to him, "Arise, go your way. Your faith has made you well."

---

[171] See appendix 6.

Exegetical idea: The ten lepers in the texts are the symbol of hope that Christ brought to those marginalized and discriminated against because of conditions or sicknesses.

Pedagogical idea: The lepers were hopeless and desperate about their conditions, but they put their trust in Jesus and He restored them. Christian leaders can bring the same kind of hope to HIV/AIDS positive people.

Week 7: Christian Service through Love and Care

The story of the Good Samaritan is one of the greatest stories told about compassion, love, and care to be emulated by every Christian to reach out to anyone who is in need.[172] The story is about selfless, compassion, love, care, and support that Christians should be doing in the community to be like Christ. Through the lesson, the Christian leaders will be challenged, encouraged, and inspired to be compassionate in the spirit of love of Christ. The law of love rules in Christian service and the church should show that kind of compassion more than any other religion or institution. No one can love God and not love other human beings. John also mentions the kind of love that should be demonstrated by Christians in response to Christian service: "Everyone who loves has been born of God and knows God. Whoever does not love does not know God because God is love" (1 John 4:7b-9,). The key passage was Luke 10:27-30, NKJV,

> So, he answered and said, "'You shall love the Lord your God with all your heart, with all your soul, with all your strength, and with all your mind,' and 'your neighbor as yourself.'" And He said to him, "You have answered rightly; do this and you will live." But he, wanting to justify himself, said to Jesus, "And who is my neighbor?" Then Jesus answered and said: "A certain man went down from Jerusalem to Jericho, and

---

[172] See appendix 7.

fell among thieves, who stripped him of his clothing, wounded him, and departed, leaving him half dead. Now by chance a certain priest came down that road. And when he saw him, he passed by on the other side. Likewise, a Levite, when he arrived at the place, came and looked, and passed by on the other side. But a certain Samaritan, as he journeyed, came where he was. And when he saw him, he had compassion. So, he went to him and bandaged his wounds, pouring on oil and wine; and he set him on his own animal, brought him to an inn, and took care of him. On the next day, when he departed, he took out two denarii, gave them to the innkeeper, and said to him, 'Take care of him; and whatever more you spend, when I come again, I will repay you.' So, which of these three do you think was neighbor to him who fell among the thieves?" And he said, "He who showed mercy on him." Then Jesus said to him, "Go and do likewise."

Exegetical idea: The story of the Good Samaritan is about the "law of love" that is acceptable to God and man, revealing who the good neighbor is.

Pedagogical idea: A good neighbor is one who helps any person in need and assures that the person is taken care of up to the time when he is able to stand on his own; thus, it is a good lesson for all Christians.

Week 8: The Church Connecting People to God and to One Another in Fellowship and Sharing

The early church in the book of Acts demonstrates the genuine love, care, and support for every believer in the church.[173] This is the kind of love and compassion that is to be shown to all those who are in need. The lesson will teach Christian leaders to have compassion and to treat

---

[173] See appendix 8.

everyone equally because all people are equal in the eyes of God. God is compassionate, and all image-bearers must demonstrate the love God has revealed through Jesus Christ. The text teaches Christian leaders to be good examples of God's love in action in their community. The fact that the early church believers were one in heart and mind and shared everything they had equally according to need, teaches the church today to have common ground and to help each another, even those living with HIV/AIDS. The key passage is Acts 4:32-35, NKJV:

> Now the multitude of those who believed were of one heart and one soul; neither did anyone say that any of the things he possessed was his own, but they had all things in common. And with great power the apostles gave witness to the resurrection of the Lord Jesus. And great grace was upon them all. Nor was there anyone among them who lacked; for all who were possessors of lands or houses sold them and brought the proceeds of the things that were sold and laid them at the apostles' feet; and they distributed to each as anyone had need. And Joseph, who was also named Barnabas by the apostles (which is translated Son of Encouragement), a Levite of the country of Cyprus, having land, sold it, and brought the money and laid it at the apostles' feet.

Exegetical idea: The early church connected people to God and to one another in mutual relationship, prayer, fellowship, sharing, and keeping the Apostles' teachings.

Pedagogical idea: Christians in the early church demonstrated love for one another and for God by sharing possessions, praying together in fellowship, and sharing the Apostles' teachings.

Week 9: Origins of HIV/AIDS: Medical Issues

The exegesis of the texts that have been discussed highlight the biblical and the theological foundations.[174] This section brings to light theoretical facts about the hypothesis of the origins of HIV/AIDS. It sheds light on the possibility of the origins of HIV/AIDS, and discusses cultural myths of transmission, prevention, and treatment

The lesson plan will inform the Christian leaders about the possibly origins of HIV/AIDS so that they would be well-informed about HIV/AIDS. Information on transmission, prevention, and treatment was also included. With this knowledge, the leader will be able to counteract myths about transmission, prevention, and treatment. Appendix 9 contains the details of the teaching plan on the hypothesis of the possibly origins of HIV/AIDS.

Exegetical idea: The mystery of the origin of HIV/AIDS has baffled the scientists and the research is on-going.

Pedagogical idea: HIV/AIDS disease does not have any cure and it is not known from where it originated. It remains one of mysterious viruses in the history of mankind.

Week 10: Non-Medical Issues Related to HIV/AIDS

African Traditional religion and cultural norms and beliefs contribute on the spread of HIV/AIDS.[175] African culture has contributed to classifying women and children as second citizens and has promoted vulnerability to HIV/AIDS. Although no law that spells out that women and children are less privileged in African society, the culture has promoted discrimination that makes them more vulnerable than men. Christian leaders will learn how to approach African leaders to deal with the HIV/AIDS pandemic that has increased infections. Women and children are trapped in the African traditional and cultural web and there is a need for open discussion with African leaders about the culture

---

[174] See appendix 9.
[175] See appendix 10.

that jeopardizes women and children's rights. Christian leaders will develop effective responses to cultural beliefs that undermine women and children by engaging with the community leaders.

Exegetical idea: Discrimination against women and children because of cultural norms and traditions in Africa are the catalyst in spreading HIV/AIDS.

Pedagogical idea: Women and children are trapped in the African traditional and cultural web that leaves them vulnerable to HIV/AIDS infection. Christian leaders must engage with cultural and traditional leaders and teach biblical truths about equality and the rights of women and children so that they can be respected and treated with honor and dignity.

Week 11: Cultural Myths That Impact Discipleship to Those with HIV/AIDS

African cultural myths hinder discipleship, especially to those living with HIV/AIDS.[176] Cultural myths stiffen the impact of discipleship to those with HIV/AIDS. Myths about transmission do not have reasonable evidence. Social taboos are suppressive to women and are compounded by patriarchal and conservative systems that have been in force for thousands of years. The church has a great opportunity to make disciples while teaching biblical standard of living. The church incarnates into the community with the love of Christ in practical terms to transform the lives of individuals to be true disciples of Christ. The HIV/AIDS pandemic allows the church to engage with the community and provide an opportunity to serve—and in the process of serving, those who are being served may become Christians.

Exegetical idea: Cultural myths impact discipleship to those people living with HIV/AIDS in Zimbabwe.

Pedagogical idea: The church must stand against the myths that perpetuate the spread of HIV/AIDS as it stiffens the campaign against HIV/AIDS prevention and discipleship.

---

[176] See appendix 11.

Week 12: Culturally Contextualized Learner's Needs

Cultural stigma in Africa is mostly associated with shame more than guilt. The HIV/AIDS stigma boils down to isolation and depression if one discovers that he/she is infected with the disease.[177] In developing a teaching plan, women and girls must have a special place in order to meet their needs, as far as cultural and traditional norms that hinder their potential, in order to play a part in combating HIV/AIDS. Christian leaders will learn the importance of working with the community where they live to deal with HIV/AIDS cultural stigma, and at the same time, to plant seeds of hope in Christ. The biblical corrective gives hope in Christ to communities marred by cultural myths and impacted by HIV/AIDS infections. The reason the rate of HIV infections for women in Africa is rising higher than men is because women are treated inferior socially, economically, and legally due to traditional and cultural trends.

Exegetical idea: Cultural stigma in Africa is mostly associated with shame more than guilt. The HIV/AIDS stigma boils down to isolation and depression if one discovers that he/she is infected with the disease.

Pedagogical idea: HIV/AIDS affects the person who is infected, the immediate family, and the community at large, and it ultimately demands collective efforts to fight cultural stigma and shame.

Summary of Teaching Plans

The teaching lesson captures the practical action needed to accomplish the teaching plan series. The teaching plan takes into consideration learning skills, including cognitive, affective, and behavior that are needed to turn around the HIV/AIDS stigma in practical ways so that the HIV/AIDS victims can be treated with love and respect. Christians are to love one another as a sign of being in union with Christ (John 4:7-12, NKJV). Love began with God at the creation of the earth and after the fall (Gen 1:26-28, NKJV) when God reached out to His image-bearers through His sovereign grace in Christ. God's redemptive

---

[177] See appendix 12.

plan was fulfilled through the incarnation of His one and only Son, Jesus Christ (John 3:16, NKJV).

After His death and resurrection, Christ assigned His disciples to teach and disciple all nations with the Great Commission in (Matt 28:18-20, NKJV). Disciples are given the mandate to preach, teach, and disciple new converts. In the Great Commission, disciples are commissioned to teach about the restoration of those who have been isolated and shunned because of their past lives and present conditions, such as the Samaritan woman (John 4:9-19, NKJV). Furthermore, Christ gave His disciples the power and authority to heal and cast out the demons. He demonstrated His power by healing and restoring the ten lepers (Luke 17:12-19, NKJV). The Great Commission includes Christian service through loving and caring for needy people, as shown in the story of the Good Samaritan who demonstrated the spirit of kindness and love by taking care of the Jew who was robbed (Luke 10:27-30,NKJV). These texts point Christians to love and care for those living with HIV/AIDS and their need for Christ's love.

People need to be connected to God and to one another through fellowship and caring for one another. In that way, Christians are encouraged to love one another and to care and share with those amongst themselves and those on the outside (Acts 4:32-35, NKJV). The understanding of the origins and medical issues of HIV/AIDS is in the interest of Christian leaders so that they may be able to have accurate discussions with HIV/AIDS positive people. Knowledge equips Christian leaders, and those infected, to know the transmission, prevention, and treatment of the disease.

Some non-medical issues related to HIV/AIDS make women and children more vulnerable to HIV/AIDS infections because their human rights are disregarded than men's, especially in Africa. The teaching lesson points out that Christian leaders should be cognizant of African cultures and traditions and apply wisdom in order to understand cultures and how to effect change. Africa faces cultural myth challenges that impact discipleship to those with HIV/AIDS. The impact of cultural myths tends to minimize the transmission, prevention, and treatment of HIV/AIDS; however, the challenge should be pursued with diligence, wisdom, and prayer for the sake of Christ. The culturally contextualized learner's needs in which HIV/AIDS stigma is associated with shame rather than guilt when one is infected with HIV/AIDS needs to be understood in the African cultures. Those with HIV/AIDS would prefer not to disclose their HIV/AIDS status and avoid shame and guilt-conscience.

The lesson plans presented in this chapter give Christian leaders opportunities to engage with their communities to bring hope to those living with HIV/AIDS through cultural corrective and biblical corrective. The texts presented help Africa at large to engage with traditions and cultures in order to transform beliefs that do not respect women and children in a society and are vulnerable to HIV/AIDS infections.

— 5 —

CHRISTIAN LEADERSHIP TRAINING AND IMPACT

INTRODUCTION

The Christian Leadership Training Seminar will equip Christian leaders to deal with HIV/AIDS, which has affected millions of people in Africa. The training will take place in Bulawayo, a strategic central city to the many Christians leaders that are targeted for these lessons. The seminar will be advertised in local churches and para-organizations. The budget for the seminar is drafted to meet all the expenses to be incurred. Follow up steps will be taken for the Christian leaders to give a feedback and evaluate the course.

The feedback from the Christian leaders will help to assess the strengths and weaknesses of the course, thus giving the leadership the opportunity to improve the course. Consequently, modifications would improve the quality of the course. The anticipated outcomes will vindicate the cause of the Christian leadership training seminar.

Location

The venue for the seminars will be the Gasela International Counseling & Leadership Center (GICLC) in Bulawayo, the second largest city in the country. It is an industrial city. GICLC is a well-known institution for higher learning in theological and educational training for Christian leaders. It is strategically located and easily accessible by road and air. As a former student of the college, I have a strong connection with the leadership of the school, which will result in reasonable discounts for the seminars. There is adequate accommodation for housing the 25 Christians leaders and they will pay a minimum charge to cover the costs of the seminar. Lunch, breakfast, and dinner will be provided, including snacks in between the sessions. Churches and Christian organizations will be asked to contribute and support the Christian leadership training.

Advertising and Registration

The Christian Leadership Training Seminar will be advertised in all churches through Gasela International Counseling & Leadership Center board members, in which all registered churches' information is kept. The Secretary General of GICLC meets with all pastors and Christian organizations quarterly, and he will give information to all pastors and encourage them to advertise in their respective churches. The churches will put the information in their bulletins, newsletters, websites, and in local newspaper and national TV.

The advertisement will appear on the GICLC website with registration information. Leaders will register online, or they will send the forms through the mail. There will be 25 spots available for the first quarter for the registration and the churches will choose their leaders to represent the churches.

Set-Up

GICLC will provide a lecture theater and a small classroom for group discussion. There are chairs, a projector, and a 65 inches TV in the classroom to show videos and PowerPoint for the seminars. Notebooks, paper, pens, and pencils will be provided to the participants. These supplies are in the budget of the Christian Leadership Training Seminar. Bottled water, cold drinks, coffee and tea, juice, cookies, muffins, candies, and chocolates will be provided during the seminars. Breakfast, lunch, and dinner will be provided through the GICLC cafeteria.

Follow-Up

The Christian Leaders will complete a participant evaluation form to evaluate the quality of the material provided, seminar delivery, and areas of improvements. The participant forms will be distributed to Christian leaders at the end of the seminar and they will be asked and encouraged to give honest feedback (see appendix 13). The forms will have stamped envelopes to be mailed when they have completed them in order to give the participants time to complete the forms, and to avoid bias and to be free to make honest assessments of the course. Those who might have missed sessions of the seminars will be provided with the information through the printed notes. Those with flash drives will receive a copy the material missed during sessions. For more clarification on the notes, their colleagues will be asked to help outside of class. The teacher will also be available for clarification.

There will be devotions every day in the morning before the seminars start. The seminars will have guest preachers to minister to Christian leaders every morning. The thirty-minute devotions are meant to encourage and inspire the Christian leaders to be more effective in their ministries.

FOLLOW-UP COURSES

Modifications

When the participants send back their feedback, I will assess the areas of strengths and weaknesses that they have highlighted. I will then modify the course contents and make necessary revisions. Additional research will be completed in order to make the course more effective, efficient, and relevant with quality materials that will enhance the Christian leaders' skill development for effective ministries. The course feedback will shed light on which areas of the course need improvement. After review of the feedback, a strategic plan will be made to improve the course and to take it to the next level.

Locations

The second seminar will also be offered GICLC. GICLC is a central location and will gives discounts on the cost because of my connection with them. The reason to offer the Christian leaders training seminar at GICLC for the second time is because GICLC is well-known and respected because of its conservatism and faithfulness to the belief of biblical inerrancy. The training will solidify the publicity and give Christian leaders confidence in to send more leaders for training.

The third Christian Leadership training will be held in Harare, which is the capital city of Zimbabwe. The venue will be at Gasela International Counseling & Leadership Center, which has a large hall to accommodate about thirty people. The budget will increase in Harare because it is more expensive as the capital city, although there are more Christian leaders than in Bulawayo. Two retired professors will be asked to teach the course, including myself. The material and curriculum will be given to the professors six months prior to the seminar to allow enough time to prepare for the courses and to further research on their own in order to be well versed with the courses. They will be provided with transportation, food, accommodation, and appreciation gifts.

ANTICIPATED IMPACT AND CONCLUSION

This thesis captures the anticipated vision and desire to see Christian leaders take a leading role in the challenge of HIV/AIDS in the twenty-first century with the most devastating disease that has shaken the world in general. This book began with the need to treat people living with HIV/AIDS with dignity and respect. It introduced the fundamental thesis statement that there is a God-honoring way to relate to God's image-bearers who have HIV/AIDS, and that way can be taught to Christians.

The thesis statement captures the concept of my anticipation for Christians to treat HIV/AIDS positive people in a God-honoring way. In that context, the purpose statement points to the need to develop a teaching series that would help Christians to live out the Great Commission with people living with HIV/AIDS. Teaching the concept of treating HIV/AIDS positive people with respect and dignity, from both Old and New Testaments, emphasizes the importance of all people being created in the image of God, as God image-bearers. Disciple-making is in God's mind and heart as He sought and covered the first sinners in the world (Gen 3:21, NKJV). God is the first greatest missionary, and that alone is a mandate to pursue the Great Commission with zeal and enthusiasm to make disciples of all nations (Matt 28:19-20, NKJV).

The thesis also focuses on the hypothesis of the origins of HIV/AIDS, and medical issues and non-issues related to HIV/AIDS. Cultural myths and the cultural impact have increased the spread of HIV/AIDS infections and increased the number of deaths related to the disease. This thesis gives Christian leaders the opportunity to interact with one another in group discussions, debates, and dramatization. The transmission, prevention, and treatment of HIV/AIDS is discussed in depth, highlighting the abuse perpetrated by cultural myths, which have taken advantage of vulnerable children and women in Africa because of traditions and culture. In the process, Christian leaders will have an opportunity to develop cognitively and affectively to improve their attitudes and behaviors toward people living with HIV/AIDS.

This thesis intended to open a discussion on the treatment of HIV/AIDS positive people in a God-honoring way. African cultural myths need to be addressed with cultural corrective and biblical corrective. Open discussion and dialogue among the churches, community leaders, chiefs, and headmen, should open new perceptions and reforms to enable children and women to enjoy equality and fair treatment in the community. The course should meet the anticipated needs to treat people living with HIV/AIDS in a God-honoring way. Christian leaders will be trained for twelve weeks to teach and to disseminate the information to churches and community about the need to treat HIV/AIDS positive people with respect and dignity.

FURTHER RESEARCH

Research on HIV/AIDS and the Christian response is wide and deep; therefore, further research should go deeper and further. HIV/AIDS is and continues to be a complex disease. Its origin, mutation, nature, weaknesses, and cycle continue to baffle scientists. Hypotheses about origin and nature have shed some glimpses of light.

Further HIV/AIDS research can bring relief and a permanent solution to the disease that has ravaged the continent of Africa and beyond. It has left marriages broken, orphans devastated, people hopeless, and widows and widowers perplexed and in deep sorrow and depression. The disease has caused unprecedented suffering for families, churches, and communities. Christ is the only answer and hope for those suffering from HIV/AIDS. His church should bring hope, love, and care to those living with HIV/AIDS.

THEOLOGICAL REFLECTION

Theologically, this thesis has unveiled fundamental similarities between leprosy and HIV/AIDS in terms of the stigma. There are several lessons learned from this thesis. Leaders must love people genuinely and have compassion in all situations, just as Christ demonstrated love to the lepers. Christians should love and treat all people with respect and dignity as commanded by Christ: "Greater love has no one than this that he lay down his life for his friends" (John 15:13, NKJV). Christ gave Christians a lesson to love people. HIV/AIDS church members deserve to be loved so that they can live their lives with purpose: "For the equipping the saints for the work of the ministry for building up the body of Christ" (Eph. 4:12, NKJV). Paul instructed Timothy to equip the body of Christ in Ephesus.

Christ showed the Israelites how to respond with love to people who were regarded as outcasts (Luke 17:12-19, NKJV). Christians and the church have an obligation to love and embrace church people living with HIV/AIDS. Theological reflection on a Christian response to HIV/AIDS has impacted my ministry in regard to the concept of loving, encouraging, giving, helping, and mercy demonstrated by Christ. I have been humbled by the servitude shown by the Lord Jesus Christ.

James 1:22, NKJV, challenges believers to be "doers" of the Word of God, not just "hearers." All Christians must emulate "agape love," which is sacrificial love for others as demonstrated by Christ. God's grace and faithfulness was experienced in the writing of this thesis. When God spoke with Moses, God said that He would come down and rescue the Israelites in Egypt: "The Lord said, 'I have indeed seen the misery of my people in Egypt. I have heard them crying out because of their slave drivers, and I am concerned about their suffering. So, I have come down to rescue them" (Exod. 3:7-8, NKJV). All Christians and Christian leaders must identify with people living with HIV/AIDS and be able to help them whenever they need it.

PERSONAL REFLECTION

I learned three lessons in writing this thesis. First, God is the ultimate source of love, compassion, healing, and forgiveness. As the church engages people with love and care, the love of Christ must be demonstrated in words and in actions. I have a deep passion for HIV/AIDS positive people that have been shunned, especially by the church.

All people must be treated with dignity, mutual respect, and shown the love Christ as is demonstrated in the Scriptures, regardless of their condition, situation, race, or financial situations. In the eyes of God, all people are equal, regardless of who they are or what their situations are. I have learned that people who have HIV/AIDS often have suicidal thoughts because of depression. The biblical research in this thesis strengthened my understanding of a Christian response to HIV/AIDS people and taught me how to respond in the way that Christ responded to the lepers and all outcasts in Israel. The church must have the same attitude that the Lord Jesus Christ did toward those regarded as the outcasts.

APPENDIX 1

WEEK 1: LOVING ONE ANOTHER IS A DEMONSTRATION OF GOD'S LOVE (1 JOHN 4:7-21, NKJV)

Appendix 1 is a lesson plan to teach about the love of Christ that all Christians are obligated to demonstrate love and care toward those who are the outcasts of the society and have been left out because of their HIV/AIDS status. The text teaches that Christians should love and demonstrate the love Christ by loving one other.

Date:	Location: **Gasela International Counseling & Leadership Center (GICLC), Bulawayo**	Time:
Target Group: 25 Christian Leaders from International Christian Baptist Church		
Passage: Key Scripture Passage(s), NKJV I John 4:7-21	**Cross references:** I John 3:11; John 3:16; I John 5:11; Rom. 5:8, 10; I Cor. 10:14; I John 1:18; I John 3:23; John 15:27, Luke. 2:11; I John 3:24; Eph. 3:12; Matt. 10:15; Rom. 8:15; I John 1:6; I John 2:3; Matt. 5:43; Acts 4:32-37.	
Exegetical Idea: Christians are commanded to love one another as Christ loved us, for love comes from the Father. Whoever loves is born of God and knows God.		

Pedagogical Idea: The Christian leaders will be taught about the love of God shown and demonstrated through His Son, Jesus Christ who died on the cross for our sins therefore, Christians must also demonstrate love and compassion to others.
Lesson AIM(s) **Cognitive** (Head): Christian leaders will understand the importance of treating all God's image-bearers with respect, love and care in order to correct the community on HIV/AIDS stigma.
Affective (Heart): Christian leaders will love the values being learnt about treating HIV/AIDS with dignity, respect and mutual understanding what they are going through.
Behavioral (Hands): Christian leaders will put into practice the values learnt and will completely change their attitudes and behaviors towards people living with HIV/AIDS and they will implement and apply the Biblical principles and teachings in their lives.
Hook: The Christian leaders will be asked to close their eyes and imagine the early church believers. They were one in heart and mind (32a), they were not selfish (32b), they shared their possessions (32c), they had no destitute among them (34a), they owned lands (34b) and they owned houses (34c).
Transition: The imagination of the early church will connect them to the contents of the lesson. We have discussed some applications we can employ to develop a positive attitude towards every Christian and anyone as commanded by Christ in (I John 4:7-21). The concept of love is demonstrated by applying it into our lives. Love is the gift of God deposited into our lives to make disciples, reflecting the love of Christ life?

Book: Content Outline	**Methodology**
1. Author 2. Place of writing 3. Original recipients 3. a. Internal Evidence The author of the book of I John is John son of Zebedee (Mark 1:19-20), the apostle and the author of the Gospel of John and Revelation. Another view suggests, Mary and Salome, is one and the same person.	1. Story 2. Lecture 3. Discussion

b. External Evidence	
It is quoted or referred by the early Christian writers as the undoubted writings of the apostle John. It was quoted by Pipias, Irenaeus, Cyprian and other apologists and the church fathers like Irenaeus, Clement of Alexandria, Tertullian and Origen, all designated the writer as the apostle John.	

Look: What does this part of the Bible mean to me?

In (I John 4:7-21, NKJV), John is teaching Christians to introspect and to challenge themselves and what this passage could means to them. The love that God has shown to His people should be emulated by all Christians.

DISCUSSION

1. The following questions should be answered by every Christian:

   a. Do I have the love like Christ to show others?
   b. How do you define love in relation to Christ and other fellow believers?
   c. If you profess Christ as your Lord, why is it difficult for you to love?
   d. Who is the person or people who come into your mind that you have shown love because of who they are?

2. How do you influence your family to show love in your community?

   a. Share how you communicate love in your family, church and community?
   b. Why do you think most Christians find it difficult to show love?
   c. What do you think is the main teaching in this passage and how can you apply it in your life?

Took: What will I do with this living truth?

Loving HIV/AIDS positive people it is sign that you are born of God and you love God. The procedure for solving HIV/AIDS stigma calls all Christians to love, support and care to those living with HIV/AIDS. In a group of 5, the debates about how to love HIV/AIDS positive people.

DISCUSSION

1. What do you think your attitude was like towards other people whom you do not go along with before you became a Christian compared to now after being a Christian?

    a. Do you love all Christians the same or are you still having a problem of loving other people?
    b. What do you think you should do to love people as Christ commanded us to love, especially HIV/AIDS positive?
    c. Do you have a problem of loving other people because of their race, nationality, profession or their HIV/AIDS status? What do you think you can do overcome that?

2. What events or circumstances have contributed to have that kind of attitude?

    a. Give the group about 2 minutes to discuss some of the circumstances that made them develop such attitude towards HIV/AIDS victims?

Application: John in this passage attacks Gnosticism head-on. They were circulating the false doctrine that salvation is attained by "knowledge", *gnosis*. John discusses a contrast love and knowledge of God with the gnosis ideology. If anyone says, "I love God," yet hates his brother he is a liar (vs.20a). And He has given us this command: Whoever loves God must also love his brother, (vs.21). People living with HIV/AIDS must be loved and cared by Christians. Christian leaders will put into practice what they have learned in the seminar. Loving God means loving all those God created all in His own image and loving God is knowing God because God is love.

Evaluation: The students will complete the forms to evaluate the quality of the materials of the course and the delivery.

APPENDIX 2

WEEK 2: GOD'S IMAGE-BEARERS
(GEN 1:26-28, NKJV)

The lesson plan in appendix 2 teaches about God's image-bearers. Humans were created in God's image; hence, they deserve respect and dignity. The lesson plan teaches about the image of God and how the image and likeness of God was affected by the fall and disobedience.

The students will be asked to take their seats and the will start lesson with a prayer from one of the students. The meeting will be called to order with everyone ready to start. In "God's image-bearers," we discuss the fall of mankind and reconciliation through Christ Jesus.

Date:	Location: **Gasela International Counseling & Leadership Center (GICLC), Bulawayo**	Time:
Target Group: 25 Christian Leaders from International Christian Baptist Church		
Passage: Key Scripture Passage(s), NKJV (Gen1:26-28), One of the students will read the passage.	**Cross references:** (Gen 3:1-16) Another student will read this text.	
Exegetical Idea: The fall of Adam brought misery to all mankind and there was alienation between God and man because of sin. However, through the death and the resurrection of Jesus Christ, hope, reconciliation and love has been poured out to God's image-bearers.		

Pedagogical Idea: Christian leaders will be taught that God's image-bearers who are HIV/AIDS positive must be treated with respect and dignity as God's image-bearers whom Christ died for.	
Lesson AIM(s)	
Cognitive (Head): The Christian leaders will understand the predicament of the fall and the grace of God that came through Christ Jesus.	
Affective (Heart): The Christian leaders will change their attitudes and treat the image-bearers who are living with HIV/AIDS with respect and dignity as they are God's image-bearers. They will value all God's image-bearers and develop convictions and beliefs to treat all people equally as a result of the lesson.	
Behavioral (Hands): Christian leaders will develop purposeful actions to impart to other people. Christian leaders will implement the principles learned by putting into practice what they have leaned.	
Hook: A video clip: Adam & Eve (True Story) 4thaluvofit, published on February 11, 2014.	
Transition: How do you connect the story of Adam and Eve with the sins people commit today?	

1. Discuss whether the fall affected everything in humans, including the whole image in man?
2. How is the image of God restored?
3. Discuss the visible trails of God's image in people?

Book: Content Outline	**Methodology**
1. Background of the texts 2. The image and likeness of God in man 3. The attributes of God 4. The characteristics of God in man 5. The Effects of the fall: alienation, sin and death 6. Living Hope in Christ	Ask two students to read Genesis 1:26-28, and 3:1-16. 1. Teaching (Lectures) 2. Discussion 3. Video clips 4. Slides

Look: What does the text mean to me?

Moses wrote Genesis to teach humankind that God created man, how he sinned and the aftermath of his fall.

(Gen1:26-28, NKJV), and (Gen 3:1-16, NKJV) teach us that man was created in the image of God and that through disobedience, seeking independence from God, he brought disgrace to all humanity. The image of God in all mankind was distorted and there is a call for everyone to repent (Acts 17:30). Through Adam, everyone has sinned and come short of the glory of God.

Discussion

1. What does Adam's disobedience to God's commands impact you?
2. How did Adam's sin affect all humankind and Christ's obedience did not affect all mankind?
3. How does the fall of Adam affect our lives today if we are in Christ?
4. What can motivate you as an individual to teach about God's grace shown in Christ?
5. How do you understand about faith and good works in relations to God's grace?

Took: What will I do about this truth as part of my responsibility to teach about the love of God after the fall of Adam?

Discussion

1. What are the most important things you have learned that you will take with you home and make a difference?
2. How has the teaching changed your attitudes towards HIV/AIDS positive people as God's image-bearers?
3. Given an opportunity out of the class, what will be your response when someone asks you a question about the fall of Adam and God's grace?
4. What specific actions will you take that can portray life changing attitude towards HIV/AIDS positive people as God's image-bearers?
5. Which part of the lesson that has caused you to change your behavior?

Application: The fall of Adam brought in new Adam (Christ) to give us new life.

1. The grace of God and His love brought us back to God through the death and the resurrection of Christ Jesus.
2. The gospel must be shared to all the people for the forgiveness of their sins
3. We must reflect and demonstrate the love of God and teach the grace of God
4. The last Adam compels us to teach about the love of God and to live according to His will.
5. God image-bearers are to be loved and cared even if they contract HIV/AIDS.

Evaluation: The student will be given forms to evaluate the lesson and suggest any areas of improvements.

APPENDIX 3

WEEK 3: GOD'S REDEMPTIVE PLAN FOR HUMANITY (JOHN 3:16, NKJV)

The lesson plan in appendix 3 teaches about God's redemptive plan for humanity after the fall. After Adam and Eve sinned, their relationship with God changed. God is holy and righteous. Christ Jesus came to save humanity. He was born of virgin Mary, was crucified, died, and three days later He rose from the dead. The lesson plan teaches about the love God demonstrated through His Son, Jesus Christ.

Christian leaders will interact before the class, sharing coffee and tea. After twenty minutes of fellowship, the class will be called to order to begin week 3 of the seminar.

Date:	Location: **Gasela International Counseling & Leadership Center (GICLC), Bulawayo**	Time:
Target Group: 25 Christian Leaders from International Christian Baptist Church		
Passage: (John 3:16), NKJV	**Cross references:** John 1:14,18; Isa 9:6; Rom 8:32; 2 Cor 6:18.	
Exegetical Idea: God's love was demonstrated in the death and the resurrection of Jesus Christ to give eternal life to all those who believe in Him.		

Pedagogical Idea: The love of God is the epicenter of God's love to reach out to His own people and to reconcile them to Himself as the truth to be taught to all people of the world.	
Lesson AIM(s)	
Cognitive (Head): The Christian leaders will be able to explain the love of God towards sinners by analyzing theological statements in the text.	
Affective (Heart): Christian leaders will adopt God's love toward sinners by willing to sacrifice and overlook prejudices as they teach about God's grace and love.	
Behavioral (Hands): Christian leaders will teach others to love the image-bearers as Christ loved sinners and gave His life for their redemption.	
Hook: A video clip by Chris Bryant, "A Father's Love for His Son" will introduce a lesson. The video was published on September 23, 2013, by Derek Edmond Olympic Athlete.	
Transition: After the video clip, Christian leaders will discuss the video clip in relation to Christ's love and sacrifice for sinners.	

Book: Content Outline	Methodology
1. Who is the author of this book and why did he write it? 2. The historical events surrounding the book 3. Date of its authorship and the original recipients 4. Is John 3:16 limited grace or universal grace? 5. What is Repentance, forgiveness reconciliation? 6. Justification, Sanctification and Glorification 7. Relating to HIV/AIDS victims to God's love	1. Teaching (Lecture) 2. Class Discussion 3. Discussion Groups 4. Debate on specific topics 5. Role playing 6. Use of motion pictures and video tapes 7. Use of dramatization and skits

Look: What does (John 3:16) mean to me?

This is the most quoted verse and it teaches us about God's love for humankind. As Christ loved us, Christians have an obligation to show love to God's image-bearers.

Discussion

1. John was one of the disciples of Christ and he saw how Jesus loved and lived His life selflessly.
2. The atonement proceeds from the loving heart of God.
3. Christian leaders will demonstrate the love of God by loving and getting involved in caring and support people living with HIV/AIDS.
4. What action would one take to show God's love to stigmatized HIV/AIDS positive people?
5. How would engage other people to love and care for those with HIV/AIDS?

Took: What will I do about God's love demonstrated by sending His Son to die for us our sins on the cross?

Discussion

1. What are the most important lessons learned in the text and how would you apply them?
2. Why this text is the most memorized verse in the entire Bible?
3. What teaching does text have that has changed your perspective about HIV/AIDS positive people?
4. In what ways will you teach in order to see some changes in people's attitudes?
5. In what ways does the text reflect the character of God?

Application: The love of God is seen in action in (John 3:16) and that is the pinnacle of agape love.

1. Love is not love until you give it away and Christ gave His life for sinners
2. How would you give your life for the sake of others?
3. John discusses the genuine and sacrificial love that Christians should demonstrate in order to make a difference in the community towards people living with HIV/AIDS.
4. The love we should show in both words and actions is to be put into practice.
5. In His sovereignty, God so loved and He gave His Son, therefore, all Christians must love and give their lives for Christian service.

Evaluation: The students will evaluate the lesson by filling the evaluation forms and give suggestions for improvements.

APPENDIX 4

WEEK 4: GREAT COMMISSION AND DISCIPLE MAKING (MATT 28:18-20, NKJV)

The lesson plan teaches about the Great Commission that Christ mandated His church to go and preach the Good News to all nations, proclaiming that everyone needs to repent for forgiveness of sins.

The Christian leaders will be excited about the teachings on how to respond to HIV/AIDS positive people as God's image-bearers. We will start with prayers for the class and will pray for people living with HIV/AIDS.

Date:	Location: **Gasela International Counseling & Leadership Center (GICLC), Bulawayo**	Time:
Target Group: 25 Christian Leaders from International Christian Baptist Church		
Passage: (Matt 28:18-20), NKJV	**Cross references:** Acts 2:38; Rom 6:3-4; Matt 1:23.	
Exegetical Idea: After Christ's resurrection, He commanded His disciples to make disciples of all nations. Therefore, all Christians are commissioned to make disciples of all nations teaching and baptizing them in the name of the Father, the Son and the Holy Spirit.		

Pedagogical Idea: The Great Commission compels Christians to connect with all kinds of people who need Christ's love, forgiveness and reconciliation and His compassion.
Lesson AIM(s)   **Cognitive** (Head): The Christian leaders will understand the reason of reaching out to people living with HIV/AIDS.
Affective (Heart): The Christian leaders will become compassionate toward those they are discipling who are living with HIV/AIDS.
Behavioral (Hands): The Christian leaders will begin Christ's model of discipleship to those living with HIV/AIDS.
Hook: A skit to dramatize how Christ commissioned the Great Commission to His disciples will be featured by 12 Christian leaders and one of them will act as Christ. The one who will be acting as Christ will wear a white gown and the 12 disciples will be sitting on the floor near the feet of Jesus, listening and looking at Him attentively. The one acting as Jesus will have memorized (Matt 28:18-20). This will capture the attention of the Christian leaders.   **Transition:** How do you think the disciples felt when they saw the resurrected Christ giving them the Great Commission? If you were one of them, how were you going to feel and react?   1. Get into a group of 5 and discuss what the disciples of Jesus did to accomplish what they were commanded to do?   2. What are the effective methods of discipleship and church expansion?   3. How does the church overcome the attitude from church members who do not welcome new members into the church?

Book: Content Outline	**Methodology**
1. The background of the text 2. Why did Matthew write this book? 3. What historical events surrounds this book? 4. Where was it written? Who are the original recipients and when was written? 5. The Great Commission as the mandate of the church	1. Teaching (Seminars) 2. Class Discussion 3. Debate on specific topics 4. Role playing 5. Use of motion pictures and video tapes 6. Use of dramatization, skits, and plays

7. The effective discipleship methods 8. The structure and influential church 9. The role of the church leaders to influence effective evangelism and mission in the church. 10. The Gospel, The Membership and The Mission	

Look: What does this text mean to me as a Christian leader?

The gospel of Matthew carries very important mandate for Christians to do missions to all the people in the world.

Discussion

1. What compelled God to offer His Son to be a sacrifice for sinners?
2. Why human beings do not have the love that God the Father has?
3. Why did God choose Israel to be the place where the Savior was to be born?
4. What is the contrast between the Kingdom of God and the kingdom of men?
5. Why did Jesus tell His disciples to baptize in the converts name of the Father, the Son and the Holy Spirit?
6. Why did Christ tell His disciples to remain in Jerusalem before for they would preach the good news to everyone?
7. What are the fundamental goals of Christ to send His disciples to teach all the nations what He had commanded them?
8. What are some of the teachings found in this text that you can apply to own your life?

Took: What are some of the challenges you learned about this text?

Discussion

1. What will you do out of the class about the text?
2. What specific actions will you do to accomplish the Great Commission?
3. What can motivate you to make more disciples?
4. How are you going to use the knowledge you gained in this seminar to multiple discipleship?
5. What is it that made you change your attitude towards making disciples?
6. When making disciples, what do you tell your disciples to continue to do in order to make more disciples?

Application: The Great Commission calls all Christians to teach and propagate the gospel to the ends of the earth.

1. The Great Commission compels Christians to teach and to reach out to even to those living with HIV/AIDS.
2. Discipleship means giving hope also to those who are dying of AIDS. They need the gospel of hope and comfort.

3. Christian leaders will apply what they learned in the seminar and change their behaviors to portray Christ.
4. Christian leaders will use the principles learned to multiple discipleship.
5. The Holy Spirit convicts and brings sinners to repentance

Evaluation: Give students forms to evaluate the lesson and to give suggestions for improvements.

APPENDIX 5

WEEK 5: RESTORATION AND CHRISTIAN SERVICE (JOHN 4:9-19, NKJV)

This teaching plan is about the restoration of all those who were lost but have been found and brought into the kingdom of God through Jesus Christ. People who have been socially ostracized are brought into the kingdom of God and the church in which Christ is the Head of the church, His bride.

The Samaritan woman told Jesus that He was a Jew and she was a Samaritan. She could not have given Him water to drink because Jews did not associate with Samaritans. Christ did not hold on to Jewish discrimination but instead broke social barriers.

Date:	Location: **Gasela International Counseling & Leadership Center (GICLC), Bulawayo**	Time:
Target Group: 25 Christian Leaders from International Christian Baptist Church		
Passage: (John 4:9-19), NKJV	**Cross references:** John 7:38-39; John 10:10; John 3:4;	
Exegetical Idea: Jesus' encounter with the Samaritan woman broke the cross-cultural and social barrier which existed between the Israelites and the Samaritans for centuries to show them how they should live together in harmony.		

Pedagogical Idea: Jesus overcame barriers that were based on Jewish customs and his model can be applied to the situation in the society against the discrimination against HIV/AIDS positive people.

Lesson AIM(s)

Cognitive (Head): The Christian leaders will be able to understand the barriers that existed between the Jews and the Samaritan. They will learn how Christ broke down those barriers of social discrimination against any kinds of people.

Affective (Heart): The Christian leaders will learn to be compassionate to people who experience discrimination because of their conditions or their HIV/AIDS status.

Behavioral (Hands): They will begin to assist those who are being discriminated against, and those stigmatized by their conditions or sicknesses.

Hook: One of the Christian leaders will read the text. They will discuss what their experiences have been with cultural norms in their respective areas.

Transition: After discussing their experiences of discrimination against women, we will discuss how culturally and traditionally the treatment of women. The discrimination of women in African cultural is similar to that of ancient Israel.

Book: Content Outline	Methodology
1. The authorship 2. Date and place 3. The historical background 4. What did Jesus mean by saying He is the living water? 5. Origin of enmity between the Jews and the Samaritan 6. The separation between the Jews and Samaritans on religious and commercial connection. 7. The hostility between the Jews and the Samaritan engraved with hatred and segregation. 8. The connection of the social barriers between the Jews and Samaritans with HIV/AIDS stigma	1. Teaching (Seminars) 2. Class Discussion 3. Debate on specific topics 4. Role playing 5. Use of motion pictures and video tapes 6. Use of dramatization, skits, and plays

Look: What does this text mean to me as a Christian leader?

Discussion

1. How do you relate to discrimination in your life experience?
2. How did Jesus overcome the social and religious discrimination between Israel and Samaria?
3. What do you think the Samaritan women thought when she saw a Jewish Jesus?
4. How does discrimination affects discipleship?
5. How would you overcome social and religious barriers in evangelism?
6. What does this text teaches you about discrimination of any kind?

Took: What does the text pose as a challenge for Christians to do when they see discrimination in their community?

Discussion

1. What action will you take to overcome discrimination against HIV/AIDS positive people in your community?
2. How did the Jews and the Samaritan treat women socially and religiously?
3. What have you learnt in this text that has changed your attitude towards any discrimination?
4. How would you respond to any discrimination that you can encounter?
5. What are some of the challenges you may face in teaching against HIV/AIDS discrimination?

Application: List seven things that you will do differently after this class and how you may do it different and why?

Evaluation: The students will evaluate the content, delivery and style. They will give suggestions also about how the lesson can be improved.

APPENDIX 6

WEEK 6: RESTORATION OF THE OUTCASTS (LUKE 17:12-19, NKJV)

The lesson plan in the appendix 6 is about the restoration of the ten lepers who were the outcasts of Israel—they were driven out of the camp because of their conditions. Leprosy is the closest disease to AIDS today and the stigma associated with the disease is abhorrent. The lesson teaches about how Jesus healed and restored the ten lepers. The church must pray for and refer HIV/AIDS positive people to Jesus Christ.

The seminar on the restoration of the outcasts gives Christian leaders a glimpse of how Jesus responded to outcasts and gave them a second chance in life. The lesson will urge the participants to do better and to help those who are ostracized in society to be restored in dignity.

Date:	Location: **Gasela International Counseling & Leadership Center (GICLC), Bulawayo**	Time:
Target Group: 25 Christian Leaders from International Christian Baptist Church		
Passage: (Luke 17:12-19), NKJV	**Cross references:** Luke 10:31-33; John 4:9; Lev 13:2, 4, 45-46; Matt 9:22.	
Exegetical Idea: The ten lepers in the texts are the symbol of hope that Christ brought to those marginalized and discriminated against because of their conditions or sicknesses.		

Pedagogical Idea: The lepers were hopeless and desperate about their conditions and they put their trust in Jesus and He restored them. Christian leaders can bring the same kind of hope to HIV/AIDS positive people.

Lesson AIM(s)

Cognitive (Head): Christian leaders will understand that the outcasts face challenges from the community where they live and they will be able to teach and demonstrate Christ's love towards them.

Affective (Heart): The students will learn to be compassionate and to love those who are marginalized because of their conditions or sicknesses.

Behavioral (Hands): The Christian leaders will be able to impart the skills they have learned and they will change their behaviors positively towards helping people living with HIV/AIDS.

Hook: Three people will dramatize a skit of the prodigal son, with the father and the elder brother. They will dramatize how the prodigal son requested for his inheritance, going away and speeding his fortunes. They will show how the prodigal son returned and being restored by his father.

Transition: The restoration of the prodigal son resembles God's restoration of the outcasts who have been rejected by the society. The story also demonstrates how God restored sinners back into His kingdom after repentance.

Book: Content Outline	Methodology
1. The Authorship 2. The original recipients 3. The ten lepers restored by Jesus 4. The priests certified to examine leprosy	1. Teaching (Seminars) 2. Class Discussion 3. Debate on specific topics 4. Role playing 5. Use of motion pictures and video tapes 6. Use of dramatization, skits, plays

Look: What does the text teach us as Christian leaders and on how to respond to all kinds of people in need?

Discussion

1. What are some of the areas of your strengths regarding helping those people facing discriminating because of their conditions?
2. With the ten lepers approaching Jesus, how did He respond to their request?

3. How did the lepers respond to Jesus' instructions?
4. In what ways can you apply the same faith and obedience in your life when instructed to do something you need?
5. How will you be involved in your church and community to help those who are HIV/AIDS positive?
6. What motivates you to be part of the agent of change in the community?

Took: What is your strategic plan to implement what you have learned in this seminar?

Discussion

1. What steps are you going to take to make sure you are on track in getting involved?
2. In what ways are you going to share the knowledge you got in the seminars to help those living with HIV/AIDS in order to deal with the stigma?
3. How has the seminar changed your perception about HIV/AIDS positive people?
4. In what ways have your behavior changed and prepared now to take specific actions to achieve your goals?
5. How would you integrate the ten lepers' feelings after their healing and the HIV/AIDS positive people?

Application: Identify five things that have changed your perception about people who are discriminated because of their conditions?

How will you apply those principles you have learnt into practical reality?

Evaluation: Each student will be given a form to evaluate the lesson on the quality of the lesson and its delivery.

APPENDIX 7

WEEK 7: CHRISTIAN SERVICE THROUGH LOVE AND CARE (LUKE 10:27-30, NKJV)

The lesson plan teaches about Christian service to touch the lives of people who need help. The Good Samaritan demonstrated unconditional love and his action has a great impact from generation to generation. Christians should show and live according to God's command, such as the Good Samaritan's show of decency and love.

Date:	Location: **Gasela International Counseling & Leadership Center (GICLC), Bulawayo**	Time:
Target Group: 25 Christian Leaders from International Christian Baptist Church		
Passage: Key Scripture Passage(s), NKJV (Luke 10:27-37)	**Cross references:** Matt 22:35-40; Mark 12:28-32; Mark 12:30; Deut 6:5; Lev 19:18; Matt 12:37.	
Exegetical Idea: The story of the Good Samaritan is about the "law of love" that is acceptable to God and man, revealing who is the good neighbor.		
Pedagogical Idea: A good neighbor is the one who helps any person in need and assures that the per person is taken care of to the time when he is able to stand on his own thus it is good lesson for all Christians.		

Lesson AIM(s)
Cognitive (Head): The Christian leaders will understand the need to help those who are in need in their community and to live with a purpose to make a difference to those who are HIV/AIDS positive.
Affective (Heart): The Christian leaders will develop the spirit of Christian service to happily serve the people living with HIV/AIDS. The Christian leaders will develop the spirit of Christian service to happily serve the people living with HIV/AIDS.
Behavioral (Hands): The students will be able to apply what they have learnt in the seminar by sharing their time, resources and efforts to help those who are HIV/AIDS positive.
Hook: Five Christian leaders will dramatize the story of the Good Samaritan. One will be a robber, one will be a victim, one will be a priest, one will be a Levi and another a Good Samaritan.
Transition: The Christian leaders will discuss what the story teaches and then they will apply them to their situations.

Book: Content Outline	Methodology
1. The authorship 2. Date and place 3. The historical background 4. Context of the text 5. What lessons in the story? 6. How the story is applied to HIV/AIDS victims? 7. Love of God translates into loving image-bearers. 8. Application of the parable.	1. Dramatize the story 2. Lectures 3. Discussion

Look: What does the text say about helping people who are in need?

Discussion

1. Background of the relationship between the Samaritans and the Jews
2. How do Christian leaders relate to others who are of a different race or ethnicity?
3. What does the text teach about compassion and caring for those in need?
4. What does the text address the need to compassionate?
5. How will you get involved in serving people with HIV/AIDS?

Took: In what ways will you engage with the needy people in your community in reference to the text?

Discussion

1. How will you respond to those who are victims of stigmatization?
2. What specific steps will you take to make sure that your life has been changed by the lessons in the seminars?
3. How will you overcome the prejudice in the community you are in, regarding helping people living with HIV/AIDS?
4. How will you teach others in your church or community to change their thinking about the importance of compassion towards people who are discriminated?
5. What has changed your perception about the story of a Good Samaritan that stands out to make a difference in the community?

Application: List five things in the text that relate to you that has changed your life for the better in terms of engaging the community and treating all people equal and with great respect.

Evaluation: The Christian leaders will complete the forms to evaluate the lessons and the delivery.

APPENDIX 8

WEEK 8: THE CHURCH CONNECTING PEOPLE TO GOD AND TO ONE ANOTHER IN FELLOWSHIP AND SHARING

The lesson plan in appendix 8 discusses the importance of connecting people to God and to one another through fellowship and meeting the needs of other Christians in the household of God. The lesson plan connects the previous lesson about being a Good Samaritans to connecting people to one another through love and care.

Date:	Location: **Gasela International Counseling & Leadership Center (GICLC), Bulawayo**	Time:
Target Group: 25 Christian Leaders from International Christian Baptist Church		
Passage: Key Scripture Passage(s), NKJV (Acts 4:32-35)	**Cross references:** Acts 2:44;	
Exegetical Idea: The early church connected people to God and to one another in mutual relationship, prayer, fellowship, sharing and keeping the Apostles' teachings.		
Pedagogical Idea: Christians in the early church demonstrated the love for one another and for God by sharing the possessions they had, praying together in fellowship and teaching the Apostles' teachings.		

Lesson AIM(s)	

Cognitive (Head): The Christian leaders will understand the importance of prayer, fellowship, sharing and loving other people as demonstrated by the early church in (Acts 4:32-35).

Affective (Heart): The Christian leaders will desire to model Christian love in order to bring all people to the knowledge of Christ.

Behavioral (Hands): The Christian leaders will begin to exercise their responsibilities to teach repentance, forgiveness, fellowship, prayer, sharing and developing relationships.

Hook: Four students will read the passage and they will be some discussions of the text with everyone. They will be interactions and points of views shared as to what the text implies to today's audience.

Transition: Christian leaders will give testimonies of their experience in which they were able to use their resources to help those who were in need. They will also explain how they developed relationships with those whom they helped and how they shared the gospel with them.

Book: Content Outline	**Methodology**

1. Authorship of the book
2. Date and Place
3. Historical background
4. Unity in diversity
   in early church
5. How the Apostles maintained
   unity in the early church?
6. Biblical economics in the text
7. Response to needy people
	1. Discussion
	2. Lectures
	3. Questions and Answers

Look: What actions are you going to take after understanding the text and how are you going to apply it to your daily routine in order to help people who are in need?

1. What does the text mean to me as a Christian leader?
2. What truth can I apply in my life to be a role model?
3. What has motivated you to be a catalyst for change in the community that made you to sacrifice your life in order to develop relationships that will lead to repentance?
4. In what ways are you going to change your behavior in order to reach out to those who need your help?
5. What is it that challenged you personally that you were not doing in your Christian life before which you will start doing?

Took: What will I do with the fellowship, sharing and praying model that the early church demonstrated?

1. What specific actions you intend to take to meet the needs of your community?
2. In what ways are you going to apply the lessons you learned?
3. What are five basic things that you will take to apply?
4. How are you going to communicate the text to those who are interested in community service?
5. How did the Apostles keep the early church focused and united which you can do to motivate church planters?

Application: Identify at least three things that you can apply in your church or community from the text that will bring change and make a difference in the community.

Evaluation: The students will evaluate the quality of the lesson and the presentation by completing the evaluating forms.

APPENDIX 9

WEEK 9: ORIGINS OF HIV/AIDS: MEDICAL ISSUES

This lesson plan teaches the hypothesis of the origins of HIV/AIDS and medical issues. The origins of HIV/AIDS have been speculated and there is no concrete certainty of its origins. Students will be taught what the hypothesis are and current information on research findings. This appendix explains HIV/AIDS origins and the consequences.

Date:	Location: **Gasela International Counseling & Leadership Center (GICLC), Bulawayo**	Time:
Target Group: 25 Christian Leaders from International Christian Baptist Church		
Passage: Key Scripture Passage(s), NKJV	**Cross references:** Any Cross-Reference Passages?	
Exegetical Idea: The mystery of the origin of HIV/AIDS has baffled the scientists and the research is still on-going but they have not found its origins yet.		
Pedagogical Idea: HIV/AIDS disease does not have any cure and it is not known where it originated from and it remains one of mysterious viruses in the history of mankind.		
Lesson AIM(s) **Cognitive** (Head): The Christian leaders will understand the importance of knowing the hypothesis of the origins of HIV/AIDS. The students will be able to explain why the scientists have not yet found the origins of HIV/AIDS.		

Affective (Heart): The Christian leaders will be willing to engage in discovering the ways to prevent the spread of the HIV/AIDS. They will be able to share their feelings and experience with people living with HIV/AIDS.

Behavioral (Hands): The Christian leaders will change their perceptions about the mythical stories of HIV/AIDS that do not follow logical conclusions. Their change of behaviors towards HIV/AIDS victims will compel them to love and care for them with a deep sense of compassion.

Hook: A video clip: "*Where Did HIV Come from?*" Published on July 31, 2014, *http://on.fb.me/1rU45FP*. Will be shown and discussed in the class.

Transition: The Christian leaders will comment on the video clip about the possible origins of HIV/AIDS. They will give their own perceptions regarding their research. That discussion will lead into the lesson.

Book: Content Outline	Methodology
1. Definition of HIV and AIDS 2. The two hypotheses of the origin of HIV/AIDS 3. The infection and transmission of HIV/AIDS 4. Vulnerability to HIV/AIDS 5. The effects of HIV/AIDS stigma 6. Effective response to HIV/AIDS	1. Lectures 2. Discussion 3. Debates

A. **Look:** What do you think are the fundamental lessons about HIV/AIDS that can change people living with the disease?
1. In what ways are you going to inform people that there is no cure for HIV/AIDS that has been found?
2. What is the ultimate truth about antiviral drugs for HIV/AIDS that should be talked about in order to change lives of HIV/AIDS patient in the community?
3. How will you relate to HIV/AIDS victims that will help them understand the importance of antiviral drugs and that they don't cure?
4. How will you be involved in HIV/AIDS prevention in your community?
5. What measures are you going to take and implement in the area of HIV/AIDS stigma?

B. **Took:** In what ways are you going to be involved with people living with HIV/AIDS?

Discussion

1. What specific steps are you going to take to disseminate information about the origin of HIV/AIDS hypothesis?
2. How would you respond to people who still believe that AIDS is a hack?
3. How are you going to respond to HIV/AIDS patients who dispute about the preventions available?
4. What has changed your perception about people living with HIV/AIDS and their future?
5. In which ways are you going to be involved to decrease HIV/AIDS stigma?

Application: As a Christian leader, how are you going to participate in ways that will prevent the spread of HIV/AIDS in your community? Identify at least three action you are going to take to achieve that goal.

Evaluation: Christian leaders will evaluate the lesson for its quality and delivery by completing evaluation forms.

APPENDIX 10

WEEK 10: NON-MEDICAL ISSUES RELATED TO HIV/AIDS

The lesson plan teaches non-medical issues related to HIV/AIDS, such as women and children's vulnerability because of their treatments, especially in Africa. Often times in Africa, more women and children are infected with HIV/AIDS than men because of the traditional and cultural beliefs that put women and children as less than men.

Date:	Location: **Gasela International Counseling & Leadership Center (GICLC), Bulawayo**	Time:
Target Group: 25 Christian Leaders from International Christian Baptist Church		
Passage: Key Scripture Passage(s), NKJV	**Cross references:** Any Cross-Reference Passages?	
Exegetical Idea: Discrimination against women and children because of cultural norms and traditions in Africa are the catalyst in spreading HIV/AIDS.		
Pedagogical Idea: Women and children are trapped in the African traditional and cultural web that leave them vulnerable to HIV/AIDS infection. The Christian leaders must engage with the cultural and traditional leaders and to teach the biblical truth about equality and the rights of women and children so that they can be respected and treated with honor and dignity.		

Lesson AIM(s)
Cognitive (Head): The Christian leaders will understand how to deal with African Traditional Religions, including cultural and social realities that affect woman and children.
Affective (Heart): The students will be able to change their attitudes concerning the strategies they can make in order to dispel the prejudice and discrimination towards women and children.
Behavioral (Hands): The students will change their approach to women and children in Africa and be able to relate to them and treat them with dignity and respect. The students will develop effective responses to cultural beliefs that under minds women and children by engaging with the community leaders.
Hook: The Christian leaders will brainstorm some of the effective ways to curtail discrimination against women and children because of traditional no and cultural beliefs.
Transition: The brainstorming to find effective ways to stop discrimination against women and children will open up honest discussion about cultural barriers to elimination discrimination.

Book: Content Outline	Methodology
1. African Traditional religion beliefs 2. Human rights for women and children not working in Africa. 3. HIV/AIDS preventions that work in an Africa culture 4. HIV/AIDS transmission that do not resonate with African tradition and culture 5. HIV/AIDS treatment in a pluralized African culture	1. Discussion 2. Debates 3. Lectures

A. **Look:** What do you understand about the African tradition and culture that does not give woman and children equal status as it does to men?

Discussion

1. How are you going to engage African culture to prevent women and children from getting infected with HIV/AIDS because of their social status?

2. What are specific actions that you are planning to do to make sure that the leadership of the community fine-tunes the African traditions that promote women and children to be more vulnerable to HIV/AIDS infections?
3. How do you relate to the African culture that discriminates women and children a as long-time tradition?
4. What are your strategic plans to convince the leaders of the community to consider the open conversations about a culture that exposes women and children to HIV/AIDS infections?
5. Has your perception changed about the way the women and are treated in African culture after the lessons you have attended now than before? In what way?

B. **Took:** What will you do to make a difference in the community with what you have learned in these seminars presented?

Discussion

1. Identify specific applications in order of priority which you are going to do when you go back?
2. How are you going to mobilize your community to advocate for change in your culture and tradition for the sake of HIV/AIDS prevention to women and children?
3. What is the most important thing that has motivated you to act against discrimination of women and children in Africa?
4. Which are the areas of concern in African culture that will be difficult to change towards encouraging equality for all?
5. Personally, what has affected you concerning your culture that needs to be looked at to prevent new HIV/AIDS infections to women and children?

Application: Identify three or five strategic plans that you are going to implement that will make it easy for you to apply relating to women and children discrimination that you have learned in this seminar?

Evaluation: The Christian leaders will be asked to complete the evaluation forms to assess the quality and the delivery of the lesson.

APPENDIX 11

WEEK 11: CULTURAL MYTHS THAT IMPACT DISCIPLESHIP TO THOSE WITH HIV/AIDS

The lesson plan teaches about the cultural myths that impact discipleship with those living with HIV/AIDS.

Date:	Location: **Gasela International Counseling & Leadership Center (GICLC), Bulawayo**	Time:
Target Group: 25 Christian Leaders from International Christian Baptist Church		
Passage: Key Scripture Passage(s), NKJV	**Cross references:** Any Cross-Reference Passages?	
Exegetical Idea: The cultural myths impact discipleship to those people living with HIV/AIDS in Zimbabwe.		
Pedagogical Idea: The Church must stand against the myths that perpetuate the spread of HIV/AIDS as it stiffens the campaign against the prevention and discipleship.		
Lesson AIM(s) **Cognitive** (Head): The students will understand that unless they confront and correct the myths circulating in the country about HIV/AIDS transmission and prevent, it will not stop from spreading. The students will be able to explain the importance of understanding cultural myths and be part of the solution to dispel those myths.		

Affective (Heart): The students will be willing to engage with the community and teaching it about the false myths and how the cultural myths have influenced and promoted the spread of HIV/AIDS.

Behavioral (Hands): The students will affectionately love the people even if they are infected with HIV/AIDS and be able to teach them the genuine and true ways of HIV/AIDS prevention. The students will uphold the Christian values and attitudes towards those who are HIV/AIDS infected and be able to teach the truth about the false myths.

Hook: The class will divide into groups of fives and they will debate for and against the cultural myths for twenty minutes. Each group will report their findings and conclusions.

Transition: The reports will kick-off the discussion about the African cultural myths and how they promoted HIV/AIDS transmission and prevention.

Book: Content Outline	Methodology
1. Mythical about origin 2. Myths about transmission 3. Myths about consequences 4. Myths about prevention 5. Myths about treatment	1. Debates 2. Lectures 3. Discussion

Look: What will be your plan and goal to convince your people that cultural myths are false acclamations and should be dismissed as fallacy and delusions.

Discussion

1. What methods are you going to use to teach your community about cultural myths that claim how HIV/AIDS originated as a community curse from ancestor's spirits?
2. How are you going to convince people in your community about the false cultural myths that justifies HIV/AIDS transmissions myths?
3. What steps are you going to take to dispel the cultural myths about the HIV/AIDS consequences?
4. How are you going to teach about the true prevention of HIV/AIDS infections?
5. African traditional religion promotes herbal and encourages those infected with HIV/AIDS to consult witch-doctors for treatments, how are you going to disseminate the information about the false treatment of HIV/AIDS claims?

Took: To have effective strategic plan to apply the lessons you have learned about cultural myths on origins of HIV/AIDS, you must be prepared to use community leaders who uphold African traditional and cultural beliefs and do not want to give them up, how will you overcome this challenge?

Discussion

1. What will you do about cultural myths that have galvanized people's beliefs to deny the existence of HIV/AIDS?
2. How will you organize people in your community to teach them about HIV/AIDS prevention to dispel myths that have increased the infection?
3. What steps are you going to take to alert the community about cultural myth that says if a person has sex with a virgin, he/she will be cured of HIV/AIDS?
4. How will you bring to justice those who have sex with infants with the hope of being cured of HIV/AIDS?
5. How would you inform those who still believe that HIV/AIDS can be treated by witch-doctors?

Application: In what ways are you going to apply what you have learned in this seminar and to win your community to believe that cultural myths are delusions and human deception?

Evaluation: The Christian leaders will evaluate the presentation of the lesson and the quality of the material by filling the forms for evaluation.

APPENDIX 12

WEEK 12: CULTURALLY CONTEXTUALIZED LEARNER'S NEEDS

The lesson plan teaches the importance of understanding the culture and its belief systems. Appendix 12 teaches Christian leaders to be cautious in dealing with HIV/AIDS positive people because they will shy away because of shame from guilt.

Date:	Location: **Gasela International Counseling & Leadership Center (GICLC), Bulawayo**	Time:
Target Group: 25 Christian Leaders from International Christian Baptist Church		
Passage: Key Scripture Passage(s), NKJV	**Cross references:** Any Cross-Reference Passages?	
Exegetical Idea: Cultural stigma in Africa is mostly associated with shame more than guilt and with HIV/AIDS stigma, it boils down to isolation and depression if one discovers that he/she infected with the disease.		
Pedagogical Idea: HIV/AIDS affects the person who is infected, the immediate family and the community at large and it ultimately demands collective efforts to fight cultural stigma and shame.		

Lesson AIM(s)
Cognitive (Head): The Christian leaders will understand the importance of working together with the community where they live to deal with HIV/AIDS cultural stigma and at the same time, planting the seed of hope in Christ.
Affective (Heart): The Christian leaders will change their perceptions about cultural myths and cultural stigma about HIV/AIDS.
Behavioral (Hands): The Christian leaders will focus on the values and the attitudes that will change the community's perceptions about HIV/AIDS transmission, prevention, and treatment.
Hook: A story to hook the class: A short story about a wife whose husband left home to live with another woman. He left his home, wife and children for another woman for five years. His wife struggled to feed the children and to pay the mortgage. Eventually, she got a job and became very successful and self-sufficient. The husband was infected with HIV/AIDS and the woman whom he was living with threw him out of her home. The husband went back to ask for forgiveness from his wife and children and he was welcomed back home. They cared for him but he died two years later. The story is about the power of forgiveness and unconditional love by the abandoned wife and children who forgave him and welcomed back home and cared for him until he died. God loves us so much that He does not reject us.
Transition: The story introduces the lesson to biblical corrective in the community to teach us about the unfailing love of God and His grace even when we are the worst sinners. God is compassionate and His love is unconditional.

Book: Content Outline	**Methodology**
1. Cultural Stigma 2. Cultural Impact 3. Cultural Corrective 4. Biblical Corrective	1. Story 2. Lecture 3. Group Discussion

Look: How are you going to be involved in helping to decrease cultural HIV/AIDS stigma and shame in your community?
Discussion
1. Identify four things that has affected discipleship in your community because of cultural stigma about HIV/AIDS and what impact it has made? 2. How will you address the cultural impact of HIV/AIDS in your community?

3. List at least five strategies you will apply that you have learnt in the seminars to implement cultural corrective about HIV/AIDS?
4. How will you apply biblical correctives in a secular culture you live in?
5. How will you encourage and convince people in your community to adopt biblical truths in their lives in an effort for discipleship?

Took: The biblical corrective gives hope in Christ to the communities marred by cultural myths and impacted by HIV/AIDS infections.

Discussion

1. What actions are going to take to help people who are living with HIV/AIDS and have lost hope all together?
2. How are you going to teach biblical corrective to those who are living in a culture that does not believe in God but believes that ancestors' spirits are in control of people's lives?
3. How are you going to make disciples within the community which has a culture that is swamped by cultural myths not the truth?
4. What areas of your life have changed your perception about HIV/AIDS positive people and what plans do you have to accomplish it?

How are you going to challenge the culture that still believes in cultural myths and subsequently promotes the spread of HIV/AIDS?

Application: The students will engage their communities to participate in discussing about the HIV/AIDS transmission, prevention and treatment in order to bring change and HIV/AIDS free generation.

Evaluation: The students will evaluate the quality of the lesson and delivery by filling evaluation forms.

APPENDIX 13

CHRISTIAN LEADERS' EVALUATION FORM

Name of Evaluator_____ Date _____

Christian Response to HIV/AIDS Training Course Curriculum Evaluation Tool					
1=Insufficient 2=Requires Attention 3=Sufficient 4=Exemplary					
Criteria	1	2	3	4	Comments
Biblical Faithfulness					
The curriculum and the content are hermeneutically sound. All the Scripture is properly interpreted, explained and applied.					
The curriculum and content are theologically sound.					
Scope					
The curriculum and content sufficiently covers each issue it is designed to address.					
Methodology					
The curriculum makes use of various and appropriate learning approaches.					

Practicality					
The curriculum and content cover how to appropriately apply the Scripture to various issues.					
Behavioral Change					
The new behaviors have been developed after the course to apply them.					

APPENDIX 14

AGREEMENT TO PARTICIPATE WITH BACKGROUND INFORMATION

To be completed by 25 members of International Fellowship Baptist Church

The research that you have agreed to participate in is crucial and fundamental for Christian Response to HIV/AIDS positive members of International Fellowship Baptist Church. It requires your utmost honesty, faithfulness, and intelligence in order to reach the desired goals and objectives. The information provided will be strictly confidential and kept safe.

Check or fill your response on the space provided.

1. Age?

    a) 18-30   _____
    b) 31-40   _____
    c) 41-55   _____
    d) 56-65   _____
    e) 66+   _____

2. Gender?

    a) Male   _____
    b) Female   _____

3. Marital Status?

   a) Married _____
   b) Single _____
   c) Engaged _____

4. How many children do you have?

   a) 1 _____
   b) 2 _____
   c) 3 _____
   d) 4 _____
   e) 5 _____
   f) 6+ _____

5. Profession?

   a) White Collar Job _____
   b) Blue Collar Job _____
   c) Not working _____
   d) Retired _____

6. How long have you been a member at International Fellowship Baptist Church?

   a) Less than 1 year _____
   b) 1-2 Years _____
   c) 3-5 Years _____
   d) 6-10 years _____
   e) 10+ years _____

7. What is the level of your education?

    a) High School Diploma   _____
    b) Undergraduate   _____
    c) Postgraduate   _____
    d) Doctorate   _____

S.S.N. (last 4 Digits) _____ DATE _____

BIBLIOGRAPHY

Adams, Jay E. *Hope for the New Millenniums*. Woodruff, SC: Timeless Text, 1994.

Almond, Brenda. *AIDS-A Moral Issue: The Ethical. Legal and Social Aspects*. New York: St. Martin's Press, 1990.

Avert.org. "HIV and AIDS in Zimbabwe." Accessed June 3, 2015. www. avert.org/aids-zimbabwe.htm.

Bailey, Keith M. *Christ's Coming and His Kingdom*. Harrisburg. PA: Christian Publications, 1981.

Bock, Darrell L. *Luke*. Baker Exegetical Commentary on the New Testament, vol. 2. Grand Rapids: Baker, 1996.

Bourke, Dale Hanson. *Responding to HIV/AIDS*. Downers Grove, IL: IVP, 2013.

Burk, Denny. *The Meaning of Sex*. Wheaton, IL: Crossway, 2013.

Buttrick, George, *Interpreter's One-Volume Commentary on the Bible*. Nashville: Abingdon, 1980.

Calvin, John. *Genesis. Commentaries on the First Book of Moses*, vol. 1. Grand Rapids: Baker, 1996.

Clarke, Adam. *The Bethany Parallel Commentary on the New Testament.* Minneapolis: Bethany House, 1983.

Collins, O. Airhihenbuwa, and DeWitt J. Webster. "Culture and African Contexts of HIV/AIDS Prevention, Care and Support." *Sahara-J: Journal of Social Aspects of HIV/AIDS* 1, no. 1 (2004): 8. Accessed June 23, 2016. http://dx.doi.org/10.1080/17290376.2004.9724822.

De La Torre, Miguel. *Genesis. Belief, A Theological Commentary on the Bible.* Louisville: Westminster John Knox, 2011.

Deyoung, Kevin. *What Does the Bible Say about Homosexuality?* Wheaton, IL: Crossway, 2015.

Dube, Musa Wenkosi. *The HIV & AIDS Bible.* Chicago: University of Chicago Press, 2008.

France, R. T. *The Gospel of Matthew.* The New International Commentary on the New Testament. Grand Rapids: William B. Eerdmans, 2007.

Fretheim, Terence E. *Genesis.* In vol. 1 of *The New Interpreter's Bible Commentary in Twelve Volumes*, edited by Juliana. L. Claassens and Bruce. C. Birch, 3-1195. Nashville: Abingdon, 1994.

Frumkin, Lyn Robert, and Leonard Martin John. *Questions & Answers on AIDS.* Oradell, NJ: Medical Economics, 1987.

Gill, John. *An Exposition of First Book of Moses Called Genesis.* Lebanon, MO: Particular Baptist, 2010.

Gill, Robin. *Reflecting Theologically on AIDS: A Global Change.* London: SCM, 2007.

Hagner, Donald A. *Matthew 14-28.* Word Biblical Commentary, vol. 33B. Dallas: Word, 1995.

Haldane, James A. *Hebrews*. Newport Commentary Series. 2nd ed. Springfield, MO: Particular Baptist Press, 2002.

Hamilton, James M. *Revelation*. The Spirit Speaks to the Churches Preaching Series. Wheaton, IL: Crossway, 2012.

Hamilton, Victor P. *The Book of Genesis: Chapters 1-17*. The New International on the Old Testament. Grand Rapids: William B. Eerdmans, 1990.

Hawthorne, Gerald F., and P. Ralph Martin. *Philippians*. Word Biblical Commentary, vol. 43. Nashville: Nelson Reference and Electronic, 2004.

HIV Treatment Information Base. September 9, 2014. Accessed October 5, 2016. www.*i-base.info*.

Hodge, Charles. *2 Corinthians*. The Crossway Classic Commentaries. Wheaton, IL: Crossway, 2015.

Hodges, Jesse Wilson. *Christ's Kingdom and Coming*. Grand Rapids: Wm. B. Eerdmans, 1957.

Hoffman, Mary Ann. *Counseling Clients with HIV Disease*. New York: Guilford, 1996.

Ironside, Henry A. *I and 2 Corinthians. An Ironside Expository Commentary*. Grand Rapids: Kregel, 2006.

Jager, Hans. *AIDS and AIDS Risk Patient Care*. New York: Ellis Horwood, 1988.

Kalipeni, Ezekiel, Karen Flynn, and Cynthia Pope. *Strong Women. Dangerous Times* New York: Nova Science, 2009.

Kruse, Colin G. *2 Corinthians*. Tyndale New Testament Commentaries, vol. 8. Rev. ed. Downers Grove, IL: IVP, 2015.

Land, Helen. *A Complete Guide to Psychosocial Intervention: AIDS*. Milwaukee: Family Service America, 1992.

Leupold, Herbert C. *Exposition of Genesis: Chapters 1-19*. Christian Classics Ethereal. Grand Rapids: Baker. 1950.

Lincoln, Andrew T. *Ephesians*. Word Biblical Commentary, vol. 42. Dallas: Word, 1990.

MacArthur, John. *Romans, The MacArthur Bible Commentary*. Nashville: Thomas Nelson, 2005.

MacArthur, John. *The MacArthur New Testaments*. Chicago: Moody, 1983.

Martin, Ralph P. *Ephesians*. In vol. 2 of *The Broadman Bible Commentary*, edited by Clifton J. Allen, 1-126. Nashville: Broadman, 1971.

_____. *2 Corinthians*. Word Biblical Commentary, vol. 40. 2nd ed. Grand Rapids: Zondervan, 2014.

Mathews, Kenneth A. *Genesis 1-11:26*. The New American Commentary, vol. 1A. Nashville: Broadman & Holman, 1996.

Mbiti, John S. *Introduction to African Religion*. 2nd ed. London: Heinemann, 1991.

McKeown, James. *Genesis. Two Horizons Old Testament Commentary*. Grand Rapids: William B. Eerdmans, 2008.

Moffat, Betty Clare. *When Someone You Know Has AIDS: A Book of Hope for Family and Friends*. Santa Monica, CA: IBS, 1986.

Morris, Leon. *The Gospel according to John*. The New International Commentary on the New Testament. Rev. ed. Grand Rapids: William B Eerdmans, 1995.

Moule, Handley Carr. *Studies in Colossians and Philemon*. Grand Rapids: Kregel, 1977.

Naylor, Peter. *A Study Commentary on 2 Corinthians Chapters 1-7*. Darlington. England: Evangelical, 2002.

Nicolson, Ronald. *God in AIDS*. London: SCM, 1996.

Patterson, Paige. *Revelation*. The New American Commentary, vol. 39, Nashville: B & H, 2012.

Phillips, John. *Exploring Genesis. John Phillips Commentary*. Chicago: Moody, 1980.

_____. *Exploring Hebrews: An Expository Commentary*. Grand Rapids: Kregel, 1977.

Polhill, John B. *Acts*. The New American Commentary, vol. 26. Nashville: Broadman, 1992.

Puckett, Sam B., and Alan R. Emery. *Managing AIDS in the Workplace. Reading*. Manila, Philippines: Addison, 1988.

Quammen, David. *The Chimp and the River: How AIDS Emerged from the African Forest*. New York: W. W. Norton and Company, 2015.

Rad, Von Gerhad. *Genesis: A Commentary*. Translated by John H. Marks. Philadelphia: Westminster, 1961.

Reddish, Mitchell G. *Revelation*. Smyth and Helwys Bible Commentary. Macon, GA: Smyth and Helwys, 2001.

Reno, Russell R. *Genesis*. Brazos Theological Commentary on the Bible. Grand Rapids: Brazos, 2010.

Rice, John R. *Genesis*. "*In the Beginning . . .*" Murfreesboro, TN: Sword of the Lord, 1975.

Richard, O. Lawrence, and Gary J. Bredfeldt. *Creative Bible Teaching*. Chicago: Moody, 1998.

Richardson, Diane. *Women and AIDS*. New York: Methuen, 1988.

Richmond, Yale, and Phyllis Gestrin. *Into Africa: Intercultural Insights*. Yarmouth. ME: Intercultural, 1998.

Sacks, Robert D. *A Commentary on the Book of Genesis: Ancient Near Eastern Texts and Studies*. Vol. 6. Lewiston, Wales: Edwin Mellen, 1990.

Sailhamer, John H. *Genesis*. In vol. 1. of *The Expositor's Bible Commentary*. Edited by Frank E. Gaebelein, Walter C. Kaiser, and Richard Hess, 21-332. Grand Rapids: Zondervan. 2008.

_____. *Genesis*. In vol. 2 of *The Expositor's Bible Commentary*. Edited by Frank E. Gaebelein, 1-285. Grand Rapids: Zondervan, 1990.

Siegel, Lary. *AIDS and Substance Abuse*. New York: Haworth, 1987.

Smith, Shepherd, and Anita Moreland Smith. "Christians in the Age of AIDS." Accessed May 2, 2012. http://www.allbookstores.com/ Christians-Age-AIDS-Shepherd-Smith.

Still, Todd D. *Philippians and Philemon*. Smyth and Helwys Bible Commentary. Macon GA: Smyth and Helwys, 2011.

Taylor, Mark. *I Corinthians*. The New American Commentary, vol. 28. Nashville: B & H, 2014.

Taylor, Walter F. *Ephesians*. Augsburg Commentary on the New Testament. Minneapolis: Augsburg, 1985.

Uprichard, Harry. *A Study Commentary on Ephesians*. Darlington, England: Evangelical, 2004.

Wall, Robert W. *Colossians and Philemon*. IVP New Testament Commentary. Downers Grove, IL: IVP, 1993.

Walton, John H. *Genesis*. The NIV Application Commentary. Grand Rapids: Zondervan. 2001.

Wenham, Gordon J. *Genesis 1-15*. Word Biblical Commentary, vol. 1. Waco, TX: Word, 1987.

Wilson, Daniel. *Expository on Colossians*. *Verse-by-Verse Bible Commentary*. New York: Bible House, 1859.

Wright, Nicholas T. *Colossians and Philemon*. Tyndale New Testament Commentaries, vol. 1. Downers Grove, IL: IVP, 1986.

Printed in the United States
By Bookmasters